Men of Waugh

By the same author:
Ashes '97: Two Views from the Boundary
(with Ian Holliday)

Men of Waugh
Ashes 2001

Norman Geras

First published 2002 by Norman Geras
10 Danesmoor Rd, Manchester M20 3JS

ISBN 0 9541985 0 6 *paperback*

Produced by
Freelance Publishing Services, Brinscall, Lancs
www.freelancepublishingservices.co.uk
Printed in Great Britain by
Biddles Ltd, Guildford

CONTENTS

PREFACE

Four summers ago I followed the Ashes series between England and Mark Taylor's Australians. I went with a friend to all of the six Tests and mightily enjoyed the experience. I therefore decided to do the same again with the visit of Steve Waugh's team, and this small book is the product. It is an account of the England–Australia Tests of 2001 as I saw and reacted to them, in the company of another friend. It is not a neutral, but a partisan, account – frankly and unashamedly so. I was supporting Australia, as I have done ever since I began to take an interest in this wonderful contest at the age of eleven or twelve. Within the framework of that allegiance, I have tried to provide an informative and interesting commentary on what I saw. At the same time, this book is unlike most others covering a Test series. It is not the book of a player, sports journalist or other such member of the official cricketing intelligentsia, but a spectator's account. It tells of my experience not only of the five Test matches as they unfolded, but also of the grounds, the crowds, the ambience and other odds and ends, as well as some of what was going on in my head.

The accounts of each day's play here were generally composed first thing the following morning, though on two or three occasions I fell behind and had to complete the story of a particular day while writing up the next one. But in any event the accounts were put together more or less concurrently with the cricket they describe. At the end of each Test, I transferred what I'd written on to computer, copy-editing for clarity and economy and tidying up for style. I did not make alterations of substance with the benefit of hindsight. Readers will notice some lengthening of the coverage as the series progresses. I found it took a little time to warm to the task. But I did warm to it, and I hope I may have succeeded in communicating some of the pleasure I derived from this Ashes summer.

For each Test I have provided a scorecard and interval scores summarising the progress of the match. Series averages are appended at the end of the book, together with a few tables documenting the pattern of Australia's dominance of this contest since 1989.

My thanks are due to Piwi Eva, with whom I followed the series (our passion for the game having taken shape a long time ago in the same small corner of the globe); to Ian Holliday, my companion and co-author in 1997, who read each of my Test accounts this time round from Hong Kong and responded with helpful comments; to my wife Adèle who did the same from Manchester; and to Morris Szeftel, another friend with whom I have long shared this enthusiasm, and who read and commented on the completed manuscript. I am grateful to them for their encouragement.

Manchester, November 2001

FIRST TEST
Edgbaston
5–8 July

Scorecard

ENGLAND

M A Atherton	c M E Waugh b Gillespie	57	c M E Waugh b McGrath	4
M E Trescothick	c Warne b Gillespie	0	c M E Waugh b Warne	76
M A Butcher	c Ponting b Warne	38	c Gilchrist b Lee	41
*N Hussain	lbw b McGrath	13	retd hurt	9
I J Ward	b McGrath	23	b Lee	3
†A J Stewart	lbw b McGrath	65	c Warne b Gillespie	5
U Afzaal	b Warne	4	lbw b Gillespie	2
C White	lbw b Warne	4	b Gillespie	0
A F Giles	c Gilchrist b Warne	7	c M E Waugh b Warne	0
D Gough	c Gillespie b Warne	0	lbw b Warne	0
A R Caddick	not out	49	not out	6
Extras	(b 10, lb 8, nb 16)	34	(b 1, lb 5, nb 12)	18
Total	(65.3 overs)	294	(42.1 overs)	164

Fall of wickets 2, 106, 123, 136, 159, 170, 174, 191, 191

4, 99, 142, 148, 150, 154, 155, 155, 164

Bowling
McGrath 17.3–2–67–3
Gillespie 17–3–67–2
Lee 12–2–71–0
Warne 19–4–71–5

McGrath 13–5–34–1
Gillespie 11–2–52–3
Warne 10.1–4–29–3
M E Waugh 1–0–6–0
Lee 7–0–37–2

AUSTRALIA

M J Slater	b Gough	77
M L Hayden	c White b Giles	35
R T Ponting	lbw b Gough	11
M E Waugh	c Stewart b Caddick	49
*S R Waugh	lbw b Gough	105
D R Martyn	c Trescothick b Butcher	105
†A C Gilchrist	c Caddick b White	152
S K Warne	c Atherton b Butcher	8
B Lee	c Atherton b Butcher	0
J N Gillespie	lbw b Butcher	0
G D McGrath	not out	1
Extras	(b 3, lb 7, nb 23)	33
Total (129.4 overs)		576

Fall of wickets 98, 130, 134, 267, 336, 496, 511, 513, 513

Bowling
Gough 33–6–152–3
Caddick 36–0–163–1
White 26.4–5–101–1
Giles 25–0–108–1
Butcher 9–3–42–4

Australia won by an innings and 118 runs
Umpires: S A Bucknor and G Sharp
Toss: Australia

Progress of the match

		Lunch	*Tea*	*Close*
First day	England	106–2	191–7	294
	Australia			133–2
Second day	Australia	238–3	332–4	332–4
Third day	Australia	381–5	486–5	576
	England			48–1
Fourth day	England	154–6	164–9	

First Day

It's a day on which you can feel the approaching heat long before it arrives. I'm up at 5.00 to catch an early train to Birmingham and the air is still and close. First thing, as the train departs, I look at the morning paper, interested in anything – everything – bearing on the contest ahead. What I find is a lot of Australian confidence.

'All England's hard-earned achievements of the winter will mean bugger all when Nasser Hussain and Steve Waugh stride to the middle around 10.30am today at Edgbaston.' Thus Geoff Lawson. 'For 40 days and 40 nights since flying out of Sydney, the Australians have been not so much roaming a desert as picking their way through the wasteland that is English cricket.' Thus the *Melbourne Age*, as quoted on the same page. Underneath the headline 'Australia relaxed and ready' there is a large picture of Steve Waugh and a happy group of his team-mates, admiring the new World Test Championship trophy presented to them at Edgbaston on the previous day. True, Nasser Hussain is reported as saying that if England 'guts it out... then we can beat them, we can definitely beat them'; but this has the ring more of wanting to put up a decent fight than of real confidence in victory. Such is the prevailing atmosphere.

Well, we shall see. As always in sport I presume nothing, count on nothing. Prevailing atmosphere is as fickle as the weather. Because they have become such a formidable outfit in recent times, Australia must obviously be favourites. But England's fortunes at Test cricket have begun to change for the better, and until their poor showing in the triangular one-day competition against Pakistan and Australia this improvement had been the source of a growing hope that, just maybe, the Ashes wheel might finally be about to turn again. Australia had been beaten, too, by India in a breathtaking series turnaround on the subcontinent, so that defeat for Australia seemed a viable idea once more after their preceding sequence of 16 consecutive Test victories, the longest in the history of the game. Then, after England's failure to compete in the one-day competition, it was all doom and gloom again for a couple of weeks, but on the threshold of the Test itself the hope and the 'just maybe' seem to have returned. Me, I'll settle for a seventh successive Australian Ashes victory, having taken much pleasure from the previous six.

As the train nears Birmingham I get a call on my mobile. It's Piwi. We are booked into one of the University of Birmingham student residences and, setting out early from Hitchin, Piwi has arrived and located it. Hunter Court, he tells me, is right beside the ground at Edgbaston. A good start. I catch a cab from New Street, we check into our rooms and we're away, heading for the scene of the action. We are at the beginning of our own Ashes adventure, a summer holiday in five instalments as we follow the series day by day. This is a first for Piwi, though it is a second for me; I did the same in 1997 with another friend, Ian.

We enter the ground and just for a while it seems that it may turn out cooler than expected. There is some light cloud cover and a faint breeze. We go to our seats in the R E S Wyatt Stand and we're very happy with them. We are positioned behind deep fine leg when the bowling is from the pavilion end. Familiar old faces begin to appear: Thommo goes by; Mark Taylor is interviewed out in the middle for his view of the prospects. Steve Waugh has won the toss meanwhile and put England in to bat. The heat of the day is now upon us; it is intense, humid and plainly here to stay.

We see a remarkable first day in which 427 runs are scored – how often does that happen on the first day of a Test! – and 12 wickets fall. The battle moves this way and that, things never getting becalmed. Both sides play for the initiative; no one shuts up shop. After losing Trescothick early, England cruise past the 100 mark thanks to a century partnership between Atherton and Butcher, but just when these two seem on the point of establishing their team's hold on the day, our old friend Warne, brought on for an over before lunch, gets Butcher's wicket second ball, caught by Ponting at silly point. It is the start of a familiar sort of England procession. Between lunch and tea there is a steady fall of wickets, leaving their total wanting on 191 for 7, and with Warne bagging another two wickets immediately after tea to secure yet another five-wicket haul, England's situation has become wretched. But a quite extraordinary tenth-wicket stand between Stewart and Caddick follows; they put on 100 in 57 minutes and 73 balls. Caddick lays about him and invariably connects, and Stewart, more accustomed to this role, does the same. Spectators around us take particular pleasure in offering loud and ironic applause for Brett Lee, wicketless all day and the object of severe punishment during this partnership. McGrath finally ends it, trapping Stewart lbw.

When Australia bat, Michael Slater is plainly intent on re-possessing the initiative for his team. He takes 18 off Gough's first over, 16 of them in boundaries, and Australia take 40 from the first five. The 100 is posted in 99 balls and 70 minutes. But the dismissals of Hayden and Ponting – the former to a wonderful airborne catch by Craig White at short mid-wicket off the bowling of Ashley Giles – level things up, and the day ends more or less even.

Marvellous cricket. Sapping heat. Piwi and I have a friendly disagreement over whether Steve Waugh acted badly or well when in the recent one-day series he brought his players off the field in response to the antics of the crowd. For most of the day a lone pigeon sits out in the covers (with the bowling from the pavilion end), pecking away. Moved on from time to time by one of the players, it at once settles back to its pursuits without seeming the least bit bothered.

Second Day

Waking early on Friday I find it is much cooler and there is even moisture in the air: not substantial enough to be a drizzle, just very mild and fine but you can feel it on the face. The papers are full of the drama of the previous day and how exceptional it was for the first day of an Ashes series. Our early morning preparations completed, Piwi and I meet at 10.30, as agreed the evening before, and make our way to the ground. The lone pigeon, a two-tone black and white, is back within a couple of balls of the start. For some reason it reminds me of my cat Meems.

Today is a more traditional day of Test cricket. Slater is bowled by Gough in the latter's first over, after the addition of only a single run. The wreckage of his stumps lights up the crowd – the England supporters anyway – who are clearly hoping the dismissal might signal further positive developments. But thereafter the morning belongs to Australia. Slater's departure brings together the Waugh brothers, abreast at the starting line on nought, and they proceed to compile a century partnership, Steve looking as secure as ever and executing two or three of his trademark off-side boundaries that leave the fielders standing, Mark more slow and hesitant on this occasion. The scoring rate is not as frenetic as it was yesterday but still the 100 partnership comes up in 109 minutes. I resolve to find out how many century partnerships the Waugh twins now have together in Tests. (It turns out to be seven.)

After lunch Mark Waugh is dropped at second slip by Trescothick and the tempo changes. For a spell both batsmen have to work for their runs and they are discomfited several times by the uneven bounce in the pitch, a few deliveries skidding through low. When Mark Waugh is out caught behind off Caddick, just 29 runs have come from 14 overs since the resumption. Steve Waugh, though, bats on and on, determined, giving the bowlers and fielders nothing, choosing the delivery to dispatch contemptuously to the boundary. With Damien Martyn now partnering him, the scoring rate is pushed along again to nearly four an over, and he reaches his 26th Test century shortly before tea. I am not aware of his having given a single chance.

During the tea interval the weather begins to close in, with a build-up of dark cloud. Forty-five minutes are lost to bad light and the seeming threat of rain. Things then lighten up briefly and play resumes, but after only two balls the batsmen are offered the light and take it. Piwi and I hang about some while, inspecting the sky, wondering about the chances of a restart, debating options. We set out for our temporary pad nearby. Not nearby enough. The skies suddenly open. It is the kind of rain that leaves you drenched after just a few minutes, umbrella or no.

Australia are well-placed, ahead by 38 with six wickets in hand. If they can convert this into a substantial first-innings lead they will be sitting pretty.

Third Day

The game moved decisively Australia's way today and England have an almighty battle on their hands if they are to avoid defeat. As it was, they needed to dispose of the rest of the Australian batsmen cheaply to remain on anything like level terms. In this respect they began well enough, Waugh going in the third over of the morning lbw to Gough, with only four runs added to his score. However, two further centuries from Damien Martyn and Adam Gilchrist, the latter's an innings of stunning power, have given Australia a first innings lead of 282 and left England on the edge of a precipice.

The morning was warm and still, dry at first but with showers forecast. As Piwi and I approached our section of the Wyatt Stand we came across a sizeable gathering in front of a couple of TVs relaying the beginning of the second rugby Test between the Lions and the Wallabies. While we were taking our seats and settling down for the morning, cheers and groans, oohing and aahing, from those following the action Down Under, formed the background. The Lions had moved ahead to 11–6 by half-time, so I learned just before the start of play.

As the cricket began and Waugh departed, a couple of clowns arrived and found their seats not far from us, to be joined a bit later by two or three more. They were pretty well turned out as clowns, I thought. In the row immediately in front of us there were four Australian guys with large inflatable kangaroos that could only be accommodated by being placed on their laps. We had just about an hour's play before everyone trooped off for the light, during which time Martyn reached his 50 and the kangaroos bounced about in celebration. The bad light turned into a downpour, not lasting all that long but long enough to rule out further play for a couple of hours. Piwi and I took shelter down behind the stands and, once the storm had subsided, we made a circuit of the ground. Piwi was looking for cricketing celebrities to photograph and we did see Graham Gooch of that ilk. We also came across a large group of convicts in full uniform, and I saw a gathering of Elvis lookalikes. I picked up a 'C'mon Aussie C'mon' T-shirt from a young Australian who had just finished talking himself out of a potential difficulty with an Edgbaston merchandising official, questioning his right to be selling there. He told me, the young Australian, that the Wallabies had comfortably beaten the Lions. Grand carnival of a Test match Saturday.

On returning to our seats we were informed over the address system that lunch was being taken at the normal time, and we watched the ground staff at work clearing away the water from the extensive sheeting that had been laid down. The lone pigeon – named George by the TV commentary team, I discovered later in the day – was wandering about on top of this sheeting, cut off from its source of food.

Play eventually restarts at 2.35 and Martyn and Gilchrist add 57 in slightly better than even time, bringing up the 100 partnership between them in 98 minutes. Soon afterwards Gilchrist reaches his 50. As throughout the game so far, the runs continue to flow freely, despite clear signs that the wicket is becoming more irregular and unpredictable. The 100 for the session comes up in 90 minutes and the 150 partnership between these two batsmen just before tea, in 138 minutes. Martyn is poised on 99 and with a lead now of nearly 200 Australia are moving out of sight.

All the while a company of blokes in the rows behind us, lively from the start but whose particular style of boisterousness I have started to find intrusive since the weather and lunch break, are sounding off. One of them regularly punctuates what is a wonderful display of batting with cries of 'I'm bored' and 'I'm still bored'. They give forth humourless, repetitive obscenities. After the tea interval it becomes more ugly, as a woman in the row in front of us objects to having missiles thrown at her, only to be met with further obscenities directed specifically at her. Her husband reports this to the stewards who intervene, and things then calm down. It's the other, less savoury side of the carnival: a loutishness deep in the culture of British sport, practised in the name of innocent enjoyment, no doubt, but lamentable all the same.

Martyn brings up his hundred on the resumption, immediately follows up with a boundary and is then out to a 'relaxing', careless shot, beautifully caught by Trescothick in the gully off the bowling of Mark Butcher. His dismissal opens the gates to an hour of non-stop action, dramatic even by the standards of this match. There is first a mini-collapse by the Australian tail, the unlikely Butcher dispatching Warne, Lee and Gillespie in rapid succession to leave Australia on 513 for 9. They are reduced to this from having been on the verge of 500 for 5 and it puts Gilchrist's century in doubt. He still needs seven runs, with the not entirely reassuring figure of Glenn McGrath at the other end. Gilchrist must so arrange things as to minimise McGrath's share of the strike. In fact, not only does he reach his hundred, but the achievement triggers an astonishing display of hitting. He strikes Gough for 12 in a single over. He then hits three towering sixes off an over from Butcher, with a four thrown in for variety, though in the middle of it all Butcher misses the chance of a sharp caught and bowled. The 50 partnership between Gilchrist and McGrath is brought up in 29 minutes, McGrath's share of it nothing; and Gilchrist reaches 152 in 141 balls before being caught finally in the deep by Caddick off White. It has been an innings to match the legendary performances of Botham with the bat in 1981, and receives the generous recognition of the crowd. The Edgbaston crowd, it is appropriate to add, strikes me as all-round better behaved in 2001 than it was in 1997; suggesting – to me anyway, no neutral in this matter – that the sections of an English Test match crowd most given to behavioural excesses tend to be worse when their team is winning than when it is losing.

Be this as it may, the question of questions is now posed. Australia are all out for 576, a lead of 282. Will England crumble away or stage a battle? Will the weather intervene further, to affect the conclusion of the game? All the different elements of a possible answer are on display in what remains of the day, and for the time being we are left none the wiser. For the light intervenes in McGrath's second over and there is an interruption of 25 minutes. When the players return Atherton is out to McGrath's very next ball, caught by Mark Waugh at second slip for 4. England are 4 for 1. Trescothick and Butcher then take 37 runs from 8 overs, Warne is brought on and stems the flow with a maiden, Mark Waugh bowls a single over and the light finally puts an end to proceedings. Not long after the close of play there is another downpour. Piwi and I wonder whether or not we should check out of our rooms tomorrow morning.

Fourth Day

As the early morning is wet and it looks like we could be hanging about with little or nothing to watch, we figure we may well still need the rooms for another night. We prevaricate. It being Sunday, nobody is in the administrative office today, so we pack up our stuff as all ready to go but leave it in the rooms. In the event, play starts on time and there aren't any interruptions for the weather. The denouement is swift.

On the final day England looked for a while as though they might put up a fight. Butcher and Trescothick gave the bowling some hammer, adding 51 from the first 11 overs before Butcher was caught behind off a virtually unplayable lifting ball from Brett Lee. Butcher's 41 concluded a more than reasonable match for him with bat and ball – to say nothing of some memorably savage punishment in that one over of his to Adam Gilchrist. Brett Lee for his part, who hadn't found his rhythm in the first innings, bowled a better spell of real pace now in the second. Still, Trescothick continued to bat impressively to reach his 50. Gillespie, who also put in a fierce, accurate spell in this session, hit Hussain painfully on the hand with his first ball, and the England captain needed immediate attention from the physio; but after facing one further ball he had to retire hurt. Much well-placed hitting by Trescothick followed, lifting the run rate once more to five per over, with 95 runs having come from the first 19. George the pigeon had meanwhile returned.

Just as the tiniest seed of concern was beginning to lodge itself in my mind, England, in line with modern tradition, simply evaporated – from 143 for 2 to 164 for 9 in 23 overs either side of lunch. Ward played on to Lee and then Gillespie disposed of Stewart, Afzaal and White in short order, the first of them to a very sharp high catch by Warne at first slip. England were already busted at 154 for 6 at lunch, especially with Hussain's return now doubtful. I spoke on the phone to Adèle who had been helpfully researching trains back to Manchester for later in the day. 'There's one at 7.14,' she volunteered. '7.14?! It could be over in an hour.' It was over, in fact, after 21 minutes. To the first ball after lunch Mark Waugh spilled a chance from Giles off Gillespie, not a sight one sees very often. No matter. One run later he caught Trescothick off Warne, then Gough went lbw first ball to the same 'now-over-the-hill' fat man, making it a pair in the match for Gough, his two innings having occupied all of four balls. Warne was on a hat-trick but couldn't get past Caddick's defensive prod next ball. Finally Mark Waugh – again: his fourth catch of the game – caught Giles off Warne and it was all over. (After the Test I check out the latest catching statistics, to find that with the catches he took at

Edgbaston Waugh is now level with Allan Border on 156; he needs only two more to overtake Mark Taylor and top the record for most catches in Tests by a non-wicket-keeper.)

It immediately struck me that the result – Australia by an innings and 118 runs – strangely echoed the game at Edgbaston in 1997 when in the final innings England needed 118 to win, the exact amount of Australia's first innings total then. Moreover, as I learned from the Channel 4 highlights on my return home, an innings and 118 runs had been precisely England's winning margin over Australia at Edgbaston in 1985. A sort of double numerical revenge then. Awaiting the official presentation ceremony, Steve Waugh led his team round the ground to thank the Australian supporters, and the English fans as well, 'for their sporting behaviour', according to a report I read later. It's the first time I've seen this at cricket and I thought it was nicely done. We collected our stuff from Hunter Court and Piwi gave me a lift to New Street Station on his way through Birmingham to find a route back to Hitchin. At New Street I phoned Ian in Hong Kong; Ian who had followed the 1997 Ashes series with me, he for England, me for Australia. He wasn't home but his answering machine was. 'Aussie, Aussie, Aussie, oi, oi, oi,' I said to it, making a subtle point.

This game not only had the right result, every day of it was packed with interest: the partnership between Stewart and Caddick, seemingly out of nowhere; then Slater getting going in the Australian innings; three marvellous hundreds, Gilchrist's of a rare kind we were lucky to be present to see; the bowling of Warne, Gillespie and McGrath; and Mark Waugh, as always, at slip. There are four more Tests to go and I relish the prospect. But although England were crushed in the end, I still presume nothing.

SECOND TEST
Lord's
19–22 July

Scorecard

ENGLAND

*M A Atherton	lbw b McGrath	37		b Warne	20
M E Trescothick	c Gilchrist b Gillespie	15		c Gilchrist b Gillespie	3
M A Butcher	c M E Waugh b McGrath	21		c Gilchrist b Gillespie	83
G P Thorpe	c Gilchrist b McGrath	20		lbw b Lee	2
M R Ramprakash	b Lee	14		lbw b Gillespie	40
†A J Stewart	c Gilchrist b McGrath	0		lbw b McGrath	28
I J Ward	not out	23		c Ponting b McGrath	0
C White	c Hayden b McGrath	0		not out	27
D G Cork	c Ponting b Gillespie	24		c Warne b McGrath	2
A R Caddick	b Warne	0		c Gilchrist b Gillespie	7
D Gough	b Warne	5		c M E Waugh b Gillespie	1
Extras	(b 7, lb 8, w 2, nb 11)	28		(lb 3, w 2, nb 9)	14
Total	(63.3 overs)	187		(66 overs)	227

Fall of wickets 33, 75, 96, 121, 126, 129, 131, 178, 181

8, 47, 50, 146, 188, 188, 188, 193, 225

Bowling
McGrath 24–9–54–5
Gillespie 18–6–56–2
Lee 16–3–46–1
Warne 5.3–0–16–2

McGrath 19–4–60–3
Gillespie 16–4–53–5
Lee 9–1–41–1
Warne 20–4–58–1
M E Waugh 2–1–12–0

AUSTRALIA

M J Slater	c Stewart b Caddick	25	(2)	c Butcher b Caddick		4
M L Hayden	c Butcher b Caddick	0	(1)	not out		6
R T Ponting	c Thorpe b Gough	14		lbw b Gough		4
M E Waugh	run out	108		not out		0
*S R Waugh	c Stewart b Cork	45				
D R Martyn	c Stewart b Caddick	52				
†A C Gilchrist	c Stewart b Gough	90				
S K Warne	c Stewart b Caddick	5				
B Lee	b Caddick	20				
J N Gillespie	b Gough	9				
G D McGrath	not out	0				
Extras	(lb 9, w 1, nb 23)	33				0
Total	(101.1 overs)	401		(for 2, 3.1 overs)		14

Fall of wickets 5, 27, 105, 212, 230, 308, 322, 387, 401

6, 13

Bowling
Gough 25–3–115–3
Caddick 32.1–4–101–5
White 18–1–80–0
Cork 23–3–84–1
Butcher 3–1–12–0

Gough 2–0–5–1
Caddick 1.1–0–9–1

Australia won by 8 wickets
Umpires: S A Bucknor and J W Holder
Toss: Australia

Progress of the match

		Lunch	*Tea*	*Close*
First day	England	11–0	55–1	121–4
Second day	England	187		
	Australia		118–3	255–5
Third day	Australia	378–7	401	
	England		50–3	163–4
Fourth day	England	227		
	Australia	14–2		

First Day

Between the Tests, various issues. The first was who would captain England at Lord's with Hussain now out with a broken finger. Atherton was said initially to be reluctant, and Stewart and Butcher both ruled themselves out. Trescothick was willing and Gough too, but better not to burden the first at this early stage of a promising Test career, so the thinking was, and there is no evidence of anyone having considered the offer by Gough to be a proposition worth taking seriously. In the end Atherton agreed to do it at the England manager Duncan Fletcher's request, after taking a day's fishing to ponder the matter. On the eve of the second Test Steve Waugh was reported as being dismayed to learn that there were England players unenthusiastic about captaining their country. No Australian player, he reckoned, would have the same attitude. Dismay was it? Or a psychological ploy to diminish the opposition? This was the favoured interpretation.

A second issue was recovery from injury. Hussain was out, but would Thorpe be back? England badly needed him. And Ramprakash too, was he now fit? In the event, the news was that both would play. Three Australians – Hayden, Slater and Lee – had developed minor problems of one sort and another, but they also came through a final fitness check.

A third point in the days immediately running up to the Test was the weather. The forecast had it as unsettled for early in the week, though better by Thursday and Friday. In fact the unsettlement wasn't yet visible on Monday or Tuesday and only arrived on Wednesday. It bothered me. If the forecasters were right about the general trend and wrong about the timing, it boded ill. The first two days of the Lord's Test in 1997 had yielded no more than about an hour and a half's play and the match as a whole the equivalent of only two days' cricket. I wasn't keen on a repeat.

So much for things in the public domain. In my head I find that between Edgbaston and Lord's I am thinking about cricket – or, rather, Ashes cricket – nearly all the time. Only nearly all the time because there are the responsibilities of my job and various other demands of the reality, as opposed to the pleasure, principle. All the same I allow myself, when I can, to be preoccupied with this. I watch and re-watch some of the Channel 4 coverage of Edgbaston (in which Piwi and I make a brief appearance during the Australian circuit of the ground at the end of the match), as well as older videos from the 1997 series. Despite the technical improvements introduced to cricket coverage by Channel 4, I prefer how the Beeb used to do the evening highlights. They told a more sequential and continuous story of each day's play. I transfer my account of Edgbaston from scribbled notes on to computer. I research various features of England versus Australia in recent times – of which more later. Ashes, lovely cricket.

The day itself dawns at last and in North London where I am staying at my Dad's there is a hefty drizzle. Unable to walk to Lord's as had been my intention, I am condemned to the tube at rush hour and, more particularly, to the Northern Line which at this time of the morning is only a little better than air travel. The Jubilee Line from Baker Street to St John's Wood is better by more than that and the sense of anticipation amongst the passengers palpable. A bloke near me wearing his MCC tie is chatting to a couple of visiting Australians and his view is that, if you take away Steve Waugh and Shane Warne, there isn't too great a difference between the sides. He worries, though, that the English are no longer permitted to express national pride; and that there aren't enough good young players coming through.

At Lord's the wet conditions are at least partially compensated for by the fact that Piwi and I have the most fantastic seats, better even than the ones Ian and I had in 1997. We are beneath the Media Centre, directly behind first slip for a right-handed batsman and feel really close up to the play. Once again I am indebted to the MCC Secretary, Roger Knight, who has met our special request for tickets for all the days of the game, so as not to undermine our plan of following the entire series; and to Sarah Sienesi as well, Operations Manager in the Club Office, for being so attentive to the seating preferences I indicated. Give or take a few rows, we are in an identical position for the first four days.

The drawback is that play cannot begin. It doesn't start until 12.30 when we get just 3.2 overs before the light intervenes. Australia have won the toss again and inserted England who are 11 for 0 at what turns into a long lunch break. Play resumes at 2.30 and, with McGrath and Gillespie bowling to Atherton and Trescothick, there is an intense concentration in the air both on and off the field, the crowd as aware as the players of what is presently at stake.

The Australian close catching cordon – McGrath bowling to Atherton – is a thing of beauty. It snakes out and away from wicket-keeper Adam Gilchrist, stretching round into the gully, Shane Warne at first, and Mark Waugh at second slip, the two of them sharing a virtual uniform today, of wide-brimmed white hat, shades, short-sleeved pullover and wrist-band. Next to this laid back, two-person catching Mafia stands Ricky Ponting at third slip, and there is then a gap at fourth, followed by a second trio of Damien Martyn, Matthew Hayden and Steve Waugh. Though semi-detached from the other three, they are clearly part of the same menacing outfit. The whole positively bristles with expectation and intent.

Between lunch and another long weather break for tea Trescothick is caught by Gilchrist off Gillespie for 15, playing an uncharacteristically loose shot, and England are 33 for 1. Twice during the weather breaks Piwi and I do a circuit of Lord's round the back of the stands. Does any other cricket ground in the world attract so many spectators wearing jackets and ties? On our circuit during the tea interval we see, up on the big screen, the two teams in the pavilion being presented to the Queen. In the entire day only 40.1 overs are bowled. It is less than half a day's play, but on the other hand 40.1 more overs than Ian and I got to see on the first day here in 1997.

And it is enough time for Australia to make serious inroads on the England batting order. In the final passage of play Butcher is caught at second slip by Mark Waugh off McGrath for 21, giving Waugh his 157th catch to bring him level with Mark Taylor's record, and Atherton is lbw to the same bowler, offering no stroke. One can only wonder at the accuracy of McGrath's bowling. In his first spell he has conceded 19 runs from seven overs; in the second it is 10 runs from 8.1. On this wicket and in these conditions he is the toughest of ordeals. Shortly before the light finishes things for the day, Ramprakash is bowled between bat and pad by a beauty of a ball from Brett Lee, and England close on 121 for 4. They are in some peril unless Thorpe and Stewart can settle to a large partnership when things resume tomorrow.

Second Day

At the beginning of day two Piwi and I met at our seats and, in line with the forecast of the night before, the weather had changed. It was a nearly ideal day for watching cricket, intermittently sunny but with some light cloud cover and a fresh breeze. This meant we would not fry, and in fact we even began to feel slightly chilly in the late afternoon. The *Times* has produced a very useful *Ashes Handbook* for this series and it is being given out free at the grounds. When Piwi arrived I noticed that he had accepted yet another of these, having picked up a fair few at Edgbaston. He confessed, with some embarrassment, that this was now possibly his seventh copy. I have contented myself with two, one to keep in good shape at home for my collection, the other to shlepp to, and consult at, the grounds. If Piwi is planning to cash in on these as collectors' items, he may have some time to wait before they acquire any rarity value. I saw enormous piles of them on my way into Lord's.

McGrath continued in deadly form in the first session of play. Within 45 minutes he had accounted for Stewart and Thorpe, both caught behind, with England's score having moved along by only eight runs. For the addition of two more he had White caught by Hayden at slip, giving him a five-fer. Only after these 45 minutes, which had wrecked the bottom half of the England innings, was there a boundary, and it brought forth loud applause with a tinge of mocking irony in it. There followed a small confrontational episode between McGrath and Dominic Cork. Cork was hit on the helmet and then struck McGrath for a good six, over the head of Jason Gillespie waiting for the catch at deep long leg. And Gillespie it was in fact who got rid of Cork after he and Ward had added 47. This was through a superb catch at deep point by Ricky Ponting, falling forward to take the ball as it travelled downward at speed. Warne then wrapped up the innings, bowling Caddick and Gough in rapid sequence. 187 all out at exactly ten to one, so that the break for change of innings brought forward the lunch interval.

A different social ambience it is at Lord's, that's for sure. In the two rows behind us we had a group of City types who for the entire morning – correction, day – did not stop talking, in that loud, projected kind of voice which the self-important of this world like to be overheard in when amongst strangers. They spoke of this and that: work, investments, contacts, holidays, family and (the subject of the day) the outcome of the Jeffrey Archer trial. No 'You fat bastard' and the like here. More 'Julian', 'Christopher' and 'Annabel … absolutely vintage female'; more 'Bill, you know, who runs the advertising account at Channel 4'. The intensity and general tenor of it all shows that the cricket itself is incidental to the occasion. The main thing is the day out and the chat. The latter occasionally does take in what is happening out in the middle but with a frequency that is surprisingly low given the venue. Much less unpleasant than what we had had to endure at Edgbaston on the Saturday, it did have one link with it. By mid-afternoon a couple of these guys were issuing expressions of how very bored they were. This was in a day full of cricketing incident, including a wonderful century by one of the world's most supremely elegant batsmen.

When the Australian innings began it soon became clear that, against tight, aggressive bowling, batting would remain a challenge and that Australia had work to do to establish an advantage. They couldn't just walk away with the game. Caddick worried Matthew Hayden for four balls and then had him caught at second slip by Butcher for nought on the fifth. Ponting received a spiteful rising ball from Gough, to be taken at third slip by Thorpe. At 27 for 2 there was just the shadow of a possible crisis. Michael Slater played a cautious, watchful hand on this occasion, and he and Mark Waugh saw their side towards 50. It seemed to Piwi and me that, bringing Craig White on to bowl, Atherton moved perhaps a bit too soon towards more defensive field placings. The Australian innings anyway began to settle, Slater and

Waugh put together a 50 partnership and they brought up the 100 in 104 minutes. Mark Waugh reached his half-century looking ominously at ease from an England point of view, but Slater was then out shortly afterwards, caught behind off Caddick.

Together again now the Waugh twins and, though just after tea Steve survived a difficult chance – dropped by Gough off his own bowling – the two of them didn't take long to put Australia back on course. They compiled their second consecutive 100 partnership for the fourth wicket, their eighth century partnership overall. On the way to it they took their side past the England total of 187. There was some drama in between these two milestones, with the approach to Mark Waugh's hundred. Coming into the 90s his had been an innings of consummate class, punctuated regularly by those on-side boundaries – through mid-wicket, to square leg – which he times to perfection. Less frequent but quite majestic were two or three boundaries, also, through the covers. Despite this, the last few runs proved a minor trial for him. Part of the reason, I imagined, was Waugh's experience at Lord's in 1993 when he was bowled off his pads by Phil Tufnell when on 99. He was put to the test now by the England bowlers, Caddick in particular, bowling him short, rising deliveries, tempting him to lash out. One ball he took on the shoulder, another on the helmet. His brother even came down the wicket to offer him who knows what word of advice. Eventually he got there with a run as atypical of his innings as could be, sliced off the inside edge down to fine leg. The generous ovation of the Lord's crowd responded to the quality of the innings as against the awkward manner of its completion.

And completion this pretty well was, for a few runs later Waugh tried a quick single to Gough at deep mid-on and the Yorkshireman ran him out with a direct hit on the stumps at the bowler's end. Steve Waugh now appeared to me to become more determinedly intent on building a second large innings to follow his brother's, but on 45 he received a lifting delivery from Cork, surprising him into a catch to Stewart down the leg-side. Martyn and Gilchrist then carefully played out some ten overs or so for the addition of 25 runs. As Piwi and I returned to Hitchin it was raining again.

Third Day

The prevailing wisdom seems to be that Australia are heading for victory. The probabilities may be so, but it is obvious that England can still win this game. Walking from Piwi's house to Hitchin station in the morning, this is what we discuss. We are in complete agreement about it. Or are we? He agrees with me that an England victory is not impossible. I agree with him that it is nevertheless rather improbable. I have no real quarrel with his estimate that England have perhaps a 10% chance of victory. He seems to understand, and be amused, that even this small probability worries me.

On the last stage of our journey to Lord's, between Baker Street and St John's Wood, the carriage is crammed absolutely full. The driver of this particular Jubilee Line train is a bit of a humourist with a captive audience. He bids his passengers good morning over the intercom and surmises correctly where we are bound. He hopes England will give these kangaroos a good kickin' today, that they'll dominate the dingos, crush the koalas. Cork, he is confident, will bowl a corker, White be among the wickets and Gough and Caddick, likewise, both bring off alliterative achievements but in variants I have failed to retain. And Atherton will be at 'em. At which point our driver allows 'This is getting silly'. He will be home at 1.00, he tells us, and will watch the game on TV.

So we should make a lot of noise – unless we are members of the MCC, in which case we will just clap politely. He signs off wishing everyone a good day, and a ripple of applause passes through the carriage.

The day's play, in my perception, fell into three distinct phases. In the first two another Australian victory, and with it a virtual stranglehold over the series, seemed to move from the realm of probability towards rock-solid certainty. In the third, the nagging anxiety in my mind of there being just the outside chance of an England comeback reappeared.

During phase one, from the start of play to 40 minutes after lunch, England failed in everything they needed to succeed in to stay in the match. They did not dismiss Martyn or Gilchrist quickly and cheaply. These two raised the 50 partnership and added 50 for the morning, and then Martyn came to his own half-century, an innings that included some lovely off-side boundaries, as economical of effort as some of those we had seen the day before from Mark Waugh. Martyn was caught behind off Caddick, touching a rising ball involuntarily as he tried to take evasive action, but both before and after this dismissal a general sloppiness in the ground-fielding and catching set in for the day. Gilchrist, the real danger man for England in this situation, was dropped three times – four, according to later match reports, but one of the chances looked to me a mere quarter-chance and excusable on any day – in moving from 10 to 90, before he too was caught behind, off the bowling of Gough, immediately after lunch. He was dropped by Butcher at slip off the first ball of the second over of the day (bowled by Gough), then by Ward in the gully (off Gough again), then by Atherton at slip (off Caddick). These were all regulation catches at Test level, and the failure to accept them in a crucial session of play, did it betoken some kind of England death wish? Gilchrist for his part, given life after life, did what Gilchrist does. He thrashed the ball to all parts. Warne kept him company briefly before being caught by Stewart off Caddick – Stewart, incidentally, taking five catches in the innings – and Lee kept him company for longer, in a partnership of 50 up to lunch, making it 123 runs for the session. At that point, with the Australian lead only nine short of 200, a band set off from near where we were sitting, to play for the Saturday crowd, and the solitary drum beat with which it began sounded like nothing so much as a funeral march.

With Gilchrist out straight after lunch, England quickly wrapped up the Australian lower order, Gough and Caddick bowling Gillespie and Lee respectively. This gave Caddick 5 for 101 and, following a practice begun by the Australians – by Warne at Edgbaston and McGrath in the England first innings here – he held the ball aloft as do century-makers their bats, to mark the feat and acknowledge the crowd's applause. A bizarre confession perhaps, but safe as Australia now looked with a lead of 214, I was unhappy about the fact that their 401 was identical to the Australian first innings total at Headingley in 1981. Was a mischievous trick of fate being prepared?

Well, surely not, because in phase two, stretching from change of innings until tea, England lost three prime wickets for a mere 50 runs. Although Atherton was missed by Hayden – a difficult chance in the gully – off his first scoring shot, Gillespie soon had Trescothick caught behind, and after some slow but steady progress between Atherton and Butcher, the England captain was bowled behind his legs by Warne. On the point of tea Lee then mounted a calculated assault on Graham Thorpe with several balls about Thorpe's body as well as a dose of the verbals, culminating in a loud, successful shout for lbw. It was a brief but lethal session, phase two, sparking a discussion between Piwi and me as to whether the game would go into the fourth day. It must have laid to rest any concern about the ghostly presence of Headingley 1981.

Not necessarily. Whether or not a tinge of complacency crept into the minds of the Australians I am in no position to know. But they had, by their standards, a sloppy session in the field. A mis-field by McGrath near the boundary turned a two into a four; a shy at the wicket, not backed up in good time, yielded four more in overthrows; and further such minor misadventures occurred. Butcher and Ramprakash meanwhile stuck around towards the 50 partnership, and this was followed soon afterwards by a hefty edge over the slips to bring up 50 on Butcher's own account. One over from Shane Warne contained something approximating what would have been a beamer from a fast bowler and a further mis-field from McGrath, producing an unnecessary single. It seemed the pattern of the day, inherited by Australia from England but with less serious consequences. Butcher and Ramprakash were nearing the 100 partnership for the fourth wicket when Ramprakash was lbw to Gillespie for 40. He left the field so slowly as to suggest he must be hoping for a recall. Butcher and Stewart then saw England to stumps, with the former on a very creditable 73. England were still 51 in arrears.

Fourth Day

At breakfast Piwi and I had a follow-up discussion to the one of the previous morning. It was prompted by Vic Marks in the *Observer* who gave England no chance. Piwi on some level accepted my alternative estimate of a small chance: you know, Butcher and Stewart to add another 150 and the rest of the England batting order 50 between them, setting Australia 150-odd to win, with their patchy record, over the years, of chasing a low fourth-innings total. Yes, said Piwi, but it's only the remotest of chances. Why focus on that when all reason and knowledge point to yet another conclusive Australian victory? This is a version of the advice of Damon Runyon (I think it was): 'The race isn't always to the swift or the battle to the strong, but that's the way to bet.' Very sound, no doubt, from a betting point of view, but not Jewish enough as an outlook on life. Here it's more a matter of 'If there's a small chance something might go wrong, you'd better worry about it.' On our way into Lord's we ran across Merv Hughes who was chatting to an acquaintance and casually signing autographs. Piwi took a photo and I got Merv to sign my ticket. I was conscious suddenly of my age.

Much to everyone's surprise Steve Waugh had chosen his brother Mark to open the bowling. It worked well enough for the first over, a maiden, but Waugh's second over cost 12 runs, three boundaries well struck by Alec Stewart. That was then that, however, and no more messing; the England innings was simply taken apart. On 188 McGrath had Stewart lbw, and off the next ball induced an edge from Ward which was breathtakingly caught at third slip by Ricky Ponting. His joy and that of his team-mates overflowed. Though White survived the hat-trick ball, Butcher was caught by Gilchrist off Gillespie in the next over without addition to the total, and by way of settling a score carried over from the first innings McGrath soon dispatched Cork, caught by Warne at first slip. Four wickets had fallen in the space of three overs and five runs. White at least ensured that Australia would have to bat again, playing some impressive strokes, but the support remaining was now negligible; and Gillespie got rid of Caddick caught behind, and then Gough caught by Mark Waugh at second slip. Goodnight England. Waugh's catch took him to 158 and the new record, an achievement celebrated by him in almost balletic style as he made as if to throw the ball up in the air in front of him but released it early so that it fell away behind. Gillespie's 5 for 53 was also duly celebrated by the now established method of his holding the ball on high. It had been indeed the battle to the strong, and by just past the stroke of noon. England having made 227, Australia required 14 to win which they scored for the loss, to general merriment from the crowd, of Michael Slater and Ricky Ponting.

Australia had triumphed by 8 wickets and Glenn McGrath was nominated Man of the Match. In one way it was hard to quarrel with this verdict. I cannot recall having seen a performance as staggeringly, tormentingly, accurate as McGrath's, just putting and keeping the batsman on his mettle, ball after ball after ball: to find the right line to play down; to find a ball to score from safely; to know when to let a delivery go by; not to err. He is a fearsome contender. Yet in a game where the bowlers always had a chance of something from the wicket, we saw a golden innings by Mark Waugh, a century of fluent ease and dignity. It would have been fitting if this achievement could have been so signalled, alongside the two catches by which he overtook Mark Taylor's record. In the post-match interviews shown on the big screen Michael Atherton was asked for news about Nasser Hussain. Is he going to be fit for the third Test? 'I hope so,' said Atherton with a self-deprecatory smile, raising sympathetic laughter from the crowd.

Piwi headed off for home and I hung around a while to watch Steve Waugh take his team for a circuit of the ground, as he had done at Edgbaston, and to allow the throng departing towards St John's Wood to thin out. On the Jubilee Line down to Baker Street, a minor coincidence; it was the humourist of the morning before. 'From the sight of you all out on the platform,' he observed, 'it looks like England have got a kickin'.'

This, in truth, is what England have been getting from Australia for a good long while – since the summer of 1989. Some of the indices of Australian superiority are clear and well enough known. It is now six consecutive Ashes series, and looking like probably seven, that England have lost, and during this sequence the score in Test wins is 22 to 5 in Australia's favour. But as overwhelming as the ratio is, it actually understates the disparity. For fully four of England's five victories were achieved when the destiny of the Ashes in the series concerned had already been settled. From a sequence of 35 Tests England have won only one – at Edgbaston in 1997 – when doing so mattered to the Ashes outcome.

Another index of Australia's dominance – and this was one of the subjects of my research between the first Test and the second just concluded – is the number of times since 1989 each side has scored more than 400 in an innings. For Australia the figure is 20, with eight of those 20 innings going past 500 and four of them past 600. During the same sequence of 35 Tests England have passed 400 just four times and 500 not once. Furthermore, the Australian record of 400-plus innings is even more impressive when one looks only at the Tests played in England. I don't know why this should be, if indeed there is a reason other than mere chance. But in the 20 Ashes Tests from the four series of 1989, 1993, 1997 and 2001 so far, Australia have passed 400 in one of their innings – and sometimes they needed no more than one – 15 times. Here is the sequence of the larger (or sole) Australian innings in the Tests against England in England since 1989: 601–7 dec, 528, 424, 447, 602–6 dec, 468, 432–5 dec, 632–4 dec, 373, 653–4 dec, 408, 303, 477, 213-7 dec, 395-8 dec, 501-9 dec, 427, 220, 576, 401. These figures scarcely need further embellishment, yet it may be noted that of the five innings below 400 two were above 350, one of them an innings declared closed on 395. Is there another country with a batting performance in England anything like this one across a comparable period? It is a formidable sequence.

THIRD TEST
Trent Bridge
2–4 August

Scorecard

ENGLAND

*M A Atherton	c M E Waugh b McGrath	0		c Gilchrist b Warne	51
M E Trescothick	c Gilchrist b Gillespie	69		c Gilchrist b Warne	32
M A Butcher	c Ponting b McGrath	13		lbw b Lee	1
M R Ramprakash	c Gilchrist b Gillespie	14		st Gilchrist b Warne	26
†A J Stewart	c M E Waugh b McGrath	46		b Warne	0
I J Ward	c Gilchrist b McGrath	6		lbw b Gillespie	13
C White	c Hayden b McGrath	0		c S R Waugh b Warne	7
A J Tudor	lbw b Warne	3		c Ponting b Warne	9
R D B Croft	c Ponting b Warne	3		b Gillespie	0
A R Caddick	b Lee	13		c Gilchrist b Gillespie	4
D Gough	not out	0		not out	5
Extras	(b 1, lb 9, w 1, nb 7)	18		(b 4, lb 3, nb 7)	14
Total	(52.5 overs)	185		(57 overs)	162

Fall of wickets 0, 30, 63, 117, 142, 147, 158, 168, 180

57, 59, 115, 115, 126, 144, 144, 146, 156

Bowling
McGrath 18–4–49–5
Lee 6.5–0–30–1
Gillespie 12–1–59–2
Warne 16–4–37–2

McGrath 11–3–31–0
Gillespie 20–8–61–3
Lee 8–1–30–1
Warne 18–5–33–6

AUSTRALIA

M J Slater	b Gough	15	(2)	c Trescothick b Caddick	12
M L Hayden	lbw b Tudor	33	(1)	lbw b Tudor	42
R T Ponting	c Stewart b Gough	14		c Stewart b Croft	17
M E Waugh	c Atherton b Tudor	15		not out	42
*S R Waugh	c Atherton b Caddick	13		retd hurt	1
D R Martyn	c Stewart b Caddick	4		not out	33
†A C Gilchrist	c Atherton b Tudor	54			
S K Warne	lbw b Caddick	0			
B Lee	c Butcher b Tudor	4			
J N Gillespie	not out	27			
G D McGrath	c Butcher b Tudor	2			
Extras	(lb 3, w 1, nb 5)	9		(lb 4, nb 7)	11
Total	(54.5 overs)	190		(for 3, 29.2 overs)	158

Fall of wickets 48, 56, 69, 82, 94, 102, 102, 122, 188

36, 72, 88

Bowling
Gough 15–3–63–2
Caddick 20–4–70–3
Tudor 15.5–5–44–5
White 2–1–8–0
Croft 2–0–2–0

Gough 9–1–38–0
Caddick 12.2–1–71–1
Tudor 7–0–37–1
Croft 1–0–8–1

Australia won by 7 wickets
Umpires: J H Hampshire and S Venkataraghavan
Toss: England

Progress of the match

		Lunch	*Tea*	*Close*
First day	England	93–3	185	
	Australia			105–7
Second day	Australia	190		
	England	11–0	57–1	144–6
Third day	England	162		
	Australia	68–1	158–3	

Preamble

Well, are they or aren't they? I mean these Australians, and the best Test match side ever. It is a question in the air lately. Already four years ago – at the time of the Trent Bridge Test as it happens – several well-known commentators on the game, Ian Chappell, Matthew Engel, John Woodcock, concurred in the suggestion that the Australian side Mark Taylor had taken over from Allan Border might be fit to rank amongst the great sides of other eras. Steve Waugh's team comes down in a continuous line, obviously, from those led by his two predecessors. On the eve of the present series Mike Brearley wrote an article for *Observer Sport Monthly* comparing Waugh's men, who had strung together their sequence of 16 consecutive Test victories – a 'nearly incredible' achievement he called it – with Bradman's legendary side of 1948 and Clive Lloyd's West Indians of 1984. Brearley plumped by a narrow margin for Waugh and his team: 'They are the greatest: a match for either rival on good batting pitches, but definitely superior when the ball turns'.

This issue, it seems to me, can be dealt with in one of two ways. You can have a certain amount of fun trading argument and opinion back and forth, about this batsman as compared with that, these bowlers and those, wicket-keepers, all-rounders, fielding standards, fighting capacity in a tight spot, captaincy, morale and the kitchen sink, until conversation comes to some more or less arbitrary resting point or sets off on a different trail. Or you can assemble the relevant statistical data on the teams and the players under consideration and use these as a basis for some form of artificial game, constructed according to principles about which there will also certainly be room for disagreement. There is just such an artificial, computer-assisted game between the present Australian team and Lloyd's West Indians reported in *The Ashes: Official Guide to the first npower Test* that was on sale at Edgbaston. Apparently, the computer programme took 15 hours to run, and it had the Aussies winning by 36 runs. It is acknowledged in the article which reports this, though, that the contest is really 'too close to call … If we played it again, it's quite possible that the result would go the other way.'

By whichever method one chooses to approach it, the question provides a pleasant diversion for those of us interested in this kind of thing. Yet as a supposedly serious issue it cannot be definitively settled, and to let it agitate you doesn't seem like energy well spent. For where the statistical data leave things at all close between contending teams – and where they don't there is no question to pursue – the imponderables involved, of changing standards over time, good and bad luck with umpiring decisions or the availability of key players at key moments, as well other contextual matters, concerning, for example, whether the cricketers are to be taken as performing at the peak of their careers, or at their average level as measured over those careers, or at the level each was performing during the time relevant to assessing the team he was part of, all this will certainly create a margin for speculative judgement that exceeds the narrow gap on which the debate is focused. It is in the very nature of the question here that the two teams cannot be matched against each other over the kind of contest normal to settling it, namely, a Test series or two.

Whether this Australian side is the best ever I do not know. However, batting down to number seven with an average of 40 or better at the start of this series, and with at least two, possibly now three, batsmen who are amongst the cricketing greats, possessed likewise of a bowling attack that includes a pair of unquestionably all-time world-class bowlers, and with an outstanding catching and fielding record, as well as that sequence of 16 Test victories, they seem at least to be a legitimate subject of the question. I was therefore surprised to read an article by Frank Keating recently, delivering a loud raspberry at the very suggestion. Keating is someone whose cricket writing I generally enjoy, but this particular piece was long on sneering scepticism, long on lists of names and teams without more ado, and short on persuasive analysis and argument. Thus, he disparaged the 16 Test victories by reference to the West Indies' sequence of 29 successive series wins between 1980 and 1995, a comparison that is not to the point since the question at issue is about Steve Waugh's current team and not the relative strengths of the two cricketing powers, West Indies and Australia, over a period of a decade and a half. Again, Keating simply scoffed at the idea that this Australian attack might match those of the West Indian Supremacy, inviting his readers to pick 'any four' from Marshall, Roberts, Holding, Croft, Garner, Patterson, Ambrose and Walsh for a better quartet. Leave aside why, if it is allowed to be *any* four, we can't also throw in some of McDermott, Alderman, Lawson, Hughes, Reiffel and MacGill on the other side of the balance. The invitation backfires anyway, since great as the West Indian pace-bowling quartets of that era were, an attack that includes Warne, McGrath and Gillespie, even with the less experienced Brett Lee making up the set, will not be embarrassed by any of the invited comparisons. In fact, the four of the listed West Indian bowlers with the best combined wickets-per-Test ratio – Marshall, Roberts, Garner and Croft – come in short of the same ratio for the present Australian squad, though the margin is infinitesimally small. So also is it small when you compare composite bowling averages, again in the Australians' favour. The four Australians enjoy the advantage, furthermore, of having played some Tests in common, which these four West Indians never once did. If you take the best possible combined wickets-per-Test ratio for four from Keating's list who played together – Marshall, Holding, Garner and Croft – the margin is still tiny and in the Australians' favour, though the composite bowling average is now better for the West Indians but by the very thinnest of hairs.

It is not Frank Keating's usual mode, this mocking, curmudgeonly piece. He is more given to warm, and sometimes lavish, celebration of sporting achievement. One can't help wondering if it wasn't something other than the question overtly under discussion that was his real motivating impulse: a simple desire, perhaps, to bring Steve Waugh and the Australian camp down a peg. With this I have some sympathy. Even as an avid supporter of Australia at cricket, I have begun to tire of some of what I have read from current and former Australian players, patronising their opponents with advice on how to play to their full potential. The gap between the two sides (this style of thing goes) is not as great as it looks: England need to believe in themselves more, to be more positive and aggressive, to make their own luck, to seize the crucial opportunities each game presents them with, and so forth. It is the would-be helpful intent that is tiresome. It makes you wonder what those offering this advice – Australians after all – are really aiming at. A better, more hard-fought contest? Where they lose more games, consequently? Pull the other one. Preferable by far to me is the forthrightly partisan attitude displayed by Mark Waugh, responding to a question from his compatriot Mark Ray in a feature the latter wrote about Waugh's catching. Asked whether he had any advice to offer the England players, who have been dropping so many catches, Waugh replied: 'Advice? Keep dropping them. That's the advice'.

First Day

For Trent Bridge Australia stuck with the team that had comprehensively won the first two Tests. With Hussain not yet recovered from the injury to his hand, Atherton continued as England captain. Alex Tudor was brought in in place of Cork, and Robert Croft as an extra bowler for the injured Thorpe. I took the 7.40 train to Nottingham and on the journey tried as usual to glean what I could of opinion about the prospects. As one would expect, it was gloom again for England. A thoughtful piece by Gideon Haigh focused on their performance so far in the field. 'Watching England field this summer has been almost an act of bad taste, like reading a suicide note'. Their poor catching, according to Haigh, has not just been bad luck; it is a symptom of poor morale and poor overall showing. Mike Selvey reckoned the chances of Steve Waugh's team now cracking up were 'on the slender side of slim: Australia have never lost a series in which they have taken a 2–0 lead.' One of those mystifying facts, given out as if it possessed real power; like 'England haven't beaten Australia at Lord's since 1934'. Does it have more or less power than this other one: 'Teams have sometimes come from 2–0 down to level a series 2–2 and, on one occasion even, to win 3–2'?

But, yes, the chance of either of these things happening is very slender. All the same, if we leave aside the series outcome as a whole, I was in a position, on the basis of my recent researches, to offer England supporters the following. If the pattern of their last six losing Ashes series is any guide, England's best chance of avoiding defeat comes in the third, fourth and sixth Tests – when there is a sixth Test. Australian preponderance in the first, second and fifth Tests has been all but complete, with win-lose-(draw) ratios of, respectively, 5–1-(1), 6–0-(1) and 6–0-(0) (the first two ratios here updated to include the Tests already played in the present series). England's opportunity for a draw or a victory against the trend comes once Australia are ahead. The same ratios for the third, fourth and sixth Tests are 2–0–(4), 3–2–(1) and 0–2–(1). As is evident, England's very best chance of all comes when the fat lady has sung, gone home and gone to bed, somewhere in the vicinity of Kennington. Any power, these ratios?

Piwi phoned me on my mobile as the train was approaching Nottingham to say he had checked in for us at the student residence we had booked at Nottingham Trent University and that he would meet me off the train, which he duly did. We found parking a short walk from Trent Bridge and as we entered the ground it felt, on my third visit, like a home from home: compact in scale, relaxed, good to return to. We took our seats on the upper level of the Hound Road Stand. Once again we were delighted with the seats we had been assigned: as at Lord's, behind the slips for a right-handed batsman. A new stand has been built since I was last here, opposite our – that is, the pavilion – side of the ground. It is a long, multi-tiered structure that blocks out the whole of the Radcliffe Road end. Imposing in its way, it didn't strike me as aesthetically that impressive, bearing a resemblance to the architecture of a shopping mall.

What a day of cricket! It is the supreme beauty of this game, its great variety that confounds the most settled of expectations. From one angle it was as if there hadn't been an interval of four years since I was last at Trent Bridge. For on the final day of the England-Australia Test here in 1997, Ian and I saw 16 wickets fall. Today, Piwi and I exceeded this with a tally of 17, the last few of which brought the crowd to a pitch of excitement that must have rocked the entire neighbourhood. It was a day of wonderful bowling and mostly safe catching, in conditions, we eventually

concluded, that must be doing something for the ball pitched
on a good line and length, even though there had been talk
at the start of a very good batting strip, as is traditional to
this ground. Wickets came regularly, with only one partnership, and only one individual score, passing 50 all day.
McGrath, Gillespie and Warne all bowled beautifully –
McGrath securing another five-fer, his 20th in Tests – while
Lee continued to be rather more wayward. In their turn,
Gough, Caddick and Tudor bowled with consistency and
some spirit to put Australia in significant trouble for the
first time in the series. A young bloke next to me, one of
the more perceptive observers I have chanced to sit beside
at cricket, concluded that it was the best day of Test match
bowling he had ever watched.

Yet to begin with, it had, the day, a predictable look to it.
Though England won the toss for a change, Atherton chose
to bat first, so it was the same formula as at Edgbaston and
Lord's, and the same outcome too. For they went into a
swift decline, starting second ball when Atherton was un-
luckily given out caught by Mark Waugh at second slip off
McGrath. In fact, the ball had come off his forearm rather
than his glove. With Trescothick batting securely and impressively at his end, a steady fall set in at the other, Butcher
caught at third slip by Ponting, also off McGrath, and
Ramprakash caught behind by Gilchrist off Gillespie. There
was a 15-minute break for light rain, Trescothick reached
his half-century, McGrath at mid-off missed a chance from
Stewart off Lee and lunch intervened, before the fall proceeded. Trescothick was now caught behind off Gillespie,
and McGrath, brought back on to bowl, had Ward caught
behind off the first ball of his new spell. Then, off the last
ball of the same over, Ponting dropped a chance from White,
but it didn't matter since Hayden caught him off McGrath
soon afterwards, his score still nought. England had declined

to 147 for 6. As Martin Johnson wrote the following morning in the *Daily Telegraph*, winning the toss England had on this occasion 'elected to collapse, as opposed to being invited to do so'.

Warne was now on and, not for the first time, I took a close interest in his performance from both a bowling and a dramatic point of view. His histrionics sometimes verge on the comical. The cries and the grimaces; the shouts of 'Catch it!', now loudly articulated, now suppressed in mid-syllable as they are seen not to apply; the facial and the bodily antics accompanying virtually every ball – it all makes up quite a spectacle. But together with his enormous skill as a bowler, it may be part of the secret of Warne's success. He behaves as if he expects to take a wicket with every delivery. It reflects something about his effort and commitment and probably gets into the minds of opposing batsmen. He soon disposed of Tudor lbw, and Croft caught bat-pad by Ricky Ponting at silly point, before McGrath had Stewart gifting a catch to Mark Waugh from a lax shot outside off stump. Caddick then failed to protect his and had it knocked over by Lee. England were all out in time for tea, taken a few minutes later than usual to allow for the impending closure of the innings. It looked like the familiar story: dismissed too quickly and too cheaply.

Except that the chapter that was supposed to follow did not, though it seemed at first as if it might. Michael Slater was slow to get off the mark, but for Hayden it was Australian business as usual as he took 12 off Caddick's fourth over. The opening partnership grew towards 50. Then Tudor trapped Hayden lbw with the score on 48. Even so, Ricky Ponting started well enough with an on-driven four and, discovering a problem with his bat, signalled to the dressing room for another to be brought out. 'Get one of the English bats,' someone shouted, 'we haven't used them much.' Ye of little faith. Australia were about to take their turn and implode. Slater was bowled by Gough playing on, and Ponting, after striking two further handsome boundaries, was caught behind off the same bowler. So 69 for 3, the Waugh brothers back in town and you had to think, can they do it for a third time on the trot, the hundred-partnership routine? They could not. They did their best to dig in, to stabilise the innings. But today was a different day. The England bowlers pinned them back, making them work for every run, work just to survive. The scoring rate was throttled. In nine overs the Waughs made just 13 runs between them. Or actually not, because these runs were all scored by the older twin, while Waugh the Younger stayed put on 3, taken from a single scoring shot early in his innings. Piwi and I both thought Atherton should have a close catcher in front of the wicket for Steve Waugh facing Caddick; he was playing with some evident discomfort to the rising ball. But he was soon caught at slip anyway, by Atherton himself and off Caddick. His brother then immediately struck three fours before being caught off Tudor, same position, same fielder. Martyn fell to a catch behind and Warne was lbw, both of these also to Caddick. Australia were 102 for 7. With each dismissal the animation of the crowd was turned up a notch. Could it be true, Australia severely discountenanced at last? Widespread exhilaration at such a turn of events and me wondering if it was those ratios kicking in. A group of Australian supporters not far from us in the Hound Road Stand decided they must fly the flag, both figuratively and literally, especially now in such unaccustomed adversity. The England supporters, emboldened by what they were seeing, weren't having this. 'Get your shit stars off our flag,' some of them sang.

Play ended in what should have been the fourth last over, as the light deteriorated. After shopping for a few supplies and going for a meal, Piwi and I went back to the Clifton campus of Nottingham Trent University. Our two rooms turned out to be an exact match of the two which Ian and I had had there in 1997. As at Trent Bridge, I felt at home.

Second Day

So England went into the second day with what looked like the possibility of a good advantage on first innings, but the conclusion of Australia's was written from a different script. From somewhere they found the batting resilience that had been absent yesterday. At the centre of it was Adam Gilchrist, with only Australia's fast bowlers left to assist him. Of these Lee didn't last more than a short while before being caught by Butcher off Tudor for 4. But Gillespie stayed longer – in fact he remained undefeated. At no point, it should be emphasised, did Gilchrist try to protect him by farming the bowling. On the contrary, it happened more than once that the Australian wicket-keeper would call for a single from the first or second ball of the over or comply with one called by his partner from the last. In the circumstances the policy worried me. 'I know', I said to Piwi, 'This is about Gilchrist showing he has full confidence in Gillespie's ability to take care of himself, not undermining him. Even so …' 'It's the team ethic,' Piwi affirmed; 'there can be no exceptions.' And Gillespie did take care of himself. He accumulated singles, and a few boundaries as well, an accomplished leg-glance amongst them, while Gilchrist made do with the deliveries he had available to him. My, how Gilchrist makes do. He scored a priceless half-century, brought up in 47 balls and including 10 fours, and added 66 with Gillespie to eliminate the Australian deficit. Along the way he played some shots that just left you gaping: two luscious off-drives in one over from Gough, played either side of Ward at mid-off, who had no chance of stopping them as they raced to the boundary; a cover drive to bring up his 50 with the same clean power and velocity. In the end he was caught by Atherton off Tudor. I read later that when the partnership between them reached 50, Gillespie had faced 45 balls to Gilchrist's 18. McGrath was quickly out, superbly caught by Butcher at second slip for 2, giving Australia a lead of 5. Butcher took the catch one-handed low down to his left, and it was a fitting finale to an England catching performance that was as good here at Trent Bridge as their display at Lord's had been woeful. Tudor raised the ball in the air for an excellent comeback achievement on his part, 5 for 44.

England had three overs to face before lunch and got to the interval safely on 11 for 0, at which point the weather, predicted to be bringing sporadic storms, made an unusually well-timed intervention. It occupied the scheduled break in play and relented in time for the normal resumption, or as near as made no difference. Atherton and Trescothick proceeded in resolute fashion, seeking to lay a sound basis for a concentrated assault on Australia in the fourth innings. They were going well and had passed the 50 mark when Trescothick was out to one of those unusual dismissals that come along from time to time. He struck a ball firmly from Warne and it rebounded off the leg of Matthew Hayden, forward and close for the bat-pad catch, to be taken by the diving Gilchrist. The Australians were jubilant. Umpire Venkat called for television adjudication to satisfy himself that this was in fact how it had been, the ball not making contact with the ground. It led to the dismissal being considered controversial by some – so it was described in several papers the following morning – because the TV replay suggested the delivery should have been called a no-ball. No way controversial, I would say for my own part, since the rules as they are leave the matter of no-balls to the adjudication of the umpire. Still, along with other contested decisions in this match, it did focus attention once more on the vexed question of the relation between the umpires on the field of play and TV and other evidence, and what is the appropriate balance between them. It is a question in need of thorough review.

Even as the decision on Trescothick was being resolved, a serious downpour closed in on Trent Bridge and led to an interruption of a couple of hours, enveloping the tea interval. In a spell when the rain receded, Piwi and I walked round the ground behind the stands. We passed Paul Reiffel, and then passed him again later on. I also ran into a young Australian who had sat near us on a couple of days at Lord's. He was of the view that if England managed to win this game it would at least keep the series alive. Well, yes. Not my own inclination, however.

When play got going again, Butcher was quickly out lbw to Lee, who then hit Atherton a crunching blow on the side of his helmet, appearing to shake the England captain. But a further brief weather interruption immediately followed, so that we never discovered if he was shaken sufficiently to be brought to an early downfall. Once play resumed he and Ramprakash progressed solidly. In rapid succession, a square-cut four by Atherton brought up the 100, another by Ramprakash the 50 partnership between them and then Atherton reached his own half-century, earning warm applause for the gritty application so characteristic of him. Unhappily for England, this trio of achievements was the prelude to another disaster. Its onset had an unusual accompaniment. Into a small enclosure near the scoreboard someone had brought a very large clump of balloons some time before, which were tethered to the fence at the back. The balloons had subsequently been cut free or had simply come loose through the force of the wind, but in any case for some minutes they had been resting unstably against a thick wire that ran from ground level up on to the roof of the high building behind the scoreboard. The balloons, blue and orange, perhaps a hundred of them, perhaps more, were blowing about in the wind, manifestly not long to remain. Around Trent Bridge many eyes were fixed on them, waiting for the moment of their release. As they came free, floating up into the blue beyond to loud cheering from all sides, a leg-break from Shane Warne either passed or grazed the edge of Atherton's bat and the Australians went up for a catch behind the wicket – which umpire Venkat adjudged it was. Atherton left the field in obvious annoyance, and TV evidence soon cast doubt on Venkat's decision. To have been the victim of two wrong decisions in the same match was undeniably a misfortune, particularly with the game poised as it was at the time of this second one, and consequently much was made of it in the press. But some perspective on the thing. Earlier in the England second innings, there had been a confident shout for lbw against Atherton by McGrath. It was not upheld, leaving the bowler plainly flabbergasted. The Channel 4 highlights showed that it was out: not narrowly, but plumb; with at least as much certainty as the later caught-behind looked not to be out. The lbw appeal was turned down with England on 38. By the time Atherton went the score had moved to 115.

With his departure, the England middle order floated away in turn, ably assisted by the irrepressible Shane Warne. Attempting a cut, Stewart played a ball from Warne on to his stumps and was gone, second ball, for a duck; Ramprakash jumped out of his crease to hit Warne over the top, missed his shot and was stumped; and White gave a bat-pad catch to Steve Waugh who dived forward at silly point to scoop the ball one-handed just before it reached the ground. England had been reduced from 115 for 2 to 144 for 6.

During the same period there was a minor appearance of the Barmy Army, of which, I'm glad to say, we have seen relatively little so far during this series. Gathered mostly in one small enclosure and therefore few in number, their noise was relatively limited. But noise, basically, is what they are about. It is the only fruit of their creative powers. No humorous variation of chant or song; no melody borrowed, adapted, set to appropriate words; none of what you will get from any decent football crowd; just the same pair of words repeated monotonously and hitched to the England captain's name.

Anyway, at the business end of the day's events, Warne had finished with another five-fer, and as we set off in search of an Indian meal Piwi and I were agreed that his intervention may have shifted the balance of the game decisively in Australia's favour. This, even though they already had 140 runs to get in the final innings, plus whatever the rest of the England order could muster tomorrow, and batting hadn't looked easy for the two days so far. To us the feel of things, nevertheless, was that Australia might well reach the target unless England could increase it by a substantial margin.

We found an Indian restaurant in central Nottingham and enjoyed a good meal. As we were leaving after settling up, the proprietor, who had taken an interest in how we'd got on at the cricket, called me back to offer a gift from the restaurant: a small stone elephant. It was a nice gesture. The man could not have known that I have a collection of just such elephants on my window-sill at work. Piwi suggested that if Australia collapsed tomorrow to lose the game, I would come to see the elephant as bearing bad luck. Should this happen, I resolved, it would be left behind in my room on the Clifton campus.

Third Day

The prognosis in the morning papers tied in with our intuition of the evening before: England would need a fair few more runs to put Australia to any real trouble, a total of at least 200, possibly 250. These runs, it soon became clear, England were not going to get. Ward was lbw without addition to the overnight score, and his place in the team – like White's – must surely now be in question. Croft dragged a ball on to his stumps without scoring, and Caddick gave Gillespie his third wicket of the morning and his 100th in Tests, caught behind by Gilchrist. England were 156 for 9 after less than half an hour's play.

There was a short interruption for rain, during which Piwi and I took shelter on the enclosed staircase leading to the upper tier of the Hound Road Stand. Who should we see there, also taking shelter, but Paul Reiffel again, this time in the company of Merv Hughes. Feeling my age as I had in the same circumstances at Lord's, I asked Reiffel if he would autograph my ticket. He not only obliged but solicited Merv's signature for me as well. I thought it better to accept this a second time rather than telling them I already had it.

Tudor was out soon after play resumed, caught by Ponting in the covers off Warne, to give the blonde bombshell figures of 6 for 33. So there we were once more, at the moment that comes round regularly, when the issue is posed and everyone knows it, and if you're that way inclined – as I am – the tension grabs you and you start to mutter some quasi-imprecation, one without gods. This is what I began to do, inwardly for the most part so as not to appear to my old friend and companion in this Ashes enterprise even more irrational than he already thinks me. I began to pronounce inwardly, 'Come on, Matthew', 'Come on, Michael' – then on to Ricky and the two Waughs, and stopping, thankfully, at Damien. For never mind about England having needed 200 to 250, about the strength of this Australian team, about sensible odds and what have you. Not only was the issue now posed, it was posed for the Ashes themselves, and as Gough ran in to bowl everybody on that cricket ground who knows cricket knew that two results were still possible (discounting the draw and the tie). England might just do it. As Ian said to me later on the phone from Hong Kong, to him it looked a bit like the Oval in 1997, when Australia fell short of a 124-run target to lose by 19 runs.

'Come on, Matthew.' There were two loud lbw appeals from the first two balls of Gough's first over, the second shout a pretty good one judging by the TV replays, but both turned down. A long shaft of lightning split the sky at the Radcliffe Road end and thunder rolled across the ground. I feared the worst. But Hayden and Slater took the score into the 30s. 'Come on, Michael.' Unfortunately, Michael has for the time being lost whatever it was he had at Edgbaston; he was caught by Trescothick at third slip off Caddick for 12. Trescothick then dropped a tough chance from Hayden, who in partnership with Ponting took the score past 50. This was in the tenth over. When Hayden sent the last ball before lunch speeding to the square-leg boundary, leaving Australia on 68 for 1, the 40-minute release from tension was most welcome, as was Australia's progress encouraging thus far.

Atherton brought on Robert Croft directly after lunch and the first ball of his over Ponting hit away square on the off-side for four. But following the tendency of his innings to date in the present series, which have given only a glimpse of his capabilities with a few easy-looking boundaries be-fore he gets out, Ponting did not stay long. He got an edge off Croft's second ball and was caught behind. Croft had seemingly justified his selection thereby, because when Mark

Waugh struck him back over his head for another four off the last ball of the same over, he was taken off, having bowled only three overs in the match. Hayden was lbw to Tudor for 42 shortly afterwards and Australia had reached 88 for 3. In came Steve Waugh to join his brother. 'Come on, Steve.' From the first ball he received Waugh hit what would have been a two, but in setting off for the initial run he evidently damaged something and had to hobble to make his ground at the other end. It would later be reported that he had torn a calf muscle. He was in some pain and had to be wheeled off on a stretcher, retiring hurt. A calamity! It produced, it should be said, an ugly reaction from a proportion of the Trent Bridge crowd, who did not conceal their satisfaction.

To all appearances Steve Waugh was unlikely to come back to complete his innings, so at 89 for 3 Australia were in effect 89 for 4. The lunch-time easing of tension had been reversed. 'Come on, Mark. Come on, Damien.' Come on, especially, in view of the send-off just given to Steve Waugh. At 2.25, with the score on 97, there was another break for rain which lasted 35 minutes. Mark Waugh and Damien Martyn came back after this and batted for just 10 minutes before the rain began again, causing a further interruption. In those 10 minutes, however, the situation turned. Maybe it was only the balance between hope and worry inside me that turned. Whatever – the fact is that in those 10 minutes 20 runs of the 61 still needed were knocked off just like that, 12 of them coming in three boundaries by Martyn off successive balls from Tudor. Martyn and Waugh had taken hold of the innings and the basic arithmetic now looked to be irrecoverable for England, barring absolute meltdown. So it proved. When play resumed the batsmen needed only 25 minutes to score the remaining runs. The last of them came anti-climactically from a Caddick no-ball, without any need of a shot.

The Ashes were secure once more. Australian celebration, and relief and elation on my part. As in 1997, the Trent Bridge Test had settled the contest. Then it had been the fifth Test of six; this time it was the third of five. Then the match had gone only four days; now it lasted not even three. It ended, by an entirely suitable coincidence, on Meems's birthday. Compromising, Piwi and I stayed to watch Shane Warne collect the Man of the Match award but not to see the Australians making their post-match circuit of the ground – an act the motivation and general import of which we disagree about – and then drove back to the Clifton campus to pick up our things. Piwi made for the M1 and I for Nottingham station, a small stone elephant safely packed in my bag.

I finish here by coming back to issues concerning the best, and also the worst – the worst first. What happened on the last afternoon when Steve Waugh was injured is without any doubt one of the more unpleasant things I have seen at cricket. He was plainly in physical distress, and an appreciable section of the Trent Bridge crowd, beyond the small infestation that is the Barmy Army, took pleasure in the fact. Not to be sanctimonious about it, that England supporters – and indeed players – might have felt entitled in the situation to think that here was a piece of good fortune coming their way after all the ill luck they themselves had had with injuries, is understandable. But this was something else. It was a malicious glee, publicly expressed, at the sight of an opponent who was hurt. It was directed at Steve Waugh himself, loudly and with some venom. More than just a degree of loutishness in the sporting culture, then; on this evidence a mental thuggery that has travelled some way into England's cricketing support base.

As for the best, when I got home I 'played' Waugh's team against both Lloyd's West Indians of 1984 and Bradman's

Australians of 1948, doing so according to a method Ian and I devised during the Old Trafford Test between England and South Africa in 1998. The method consists essentially of measuring composite batting averages and composite bowling averages against one another, the bowling averages weighted to take account of combined wickets-per-Test ratios for the two attacks. Waugh's team win against Lloyd's, coming out better than it from all three of these comparisons. But they lose to Bradman's, narrowly. Without Bradman himself – even substituting for him the likes of a George Headley or Graeme Pollock, with a batting average of 60-plus – the result would go the other way. Whether or not they are the best ever, therefore, these present Australians look to be at least up there, amongst the best. However, do we really care about this, those of us who love cricket? I believe not. Despite the things by which it is demeaned, Test cricket remains for us the most absorbing and intricately beautiful of games. The statistics may contribute in some measure to the production of its enduring appeal but mainly by supplying a kind of external reassurance, a confirmation of what we see before our eyes. In the present case, the case of Waugh's Australians, it is *these players now*. To be able to sit at leisure, to watch and admire; to admire what collectively they can do, the grace and skill of top-level performance, their enjoyment of their own abilities and their enjoyment of each other's. It is this that we marvel at, this that is the substance of future memory and debate.

FOURTH TEST
Headingley
16–20 August

Scorecard

AUSTRALIA

M J Slater	lbw b Caddick	21	(2) b Gough		16
M L Hayden	lbw b Caddick	15	(1) c Stewart b Mullally		35
R T Ponting	c Stewart b Tudor	144	lbw b Gough		72
M E Waugh	c Ramprakash b Caddick	72	not out		24
D R Martyn	c Stewart b Gough	118	lbw b Caddick		6
S M Katich	b Gough	15	not out		0
*†A C Gilchrist	c Trescothick b Gough	19			
S K Warne	c Stewart b Gough	0			
B Lee	c Ramprakash b Mullally	0			
J N Gillespie	c Atherton b Gough	5			
G D McGrath	not out	8			
Extras	(b 5, lb 15, w 1, nb 9)	30	(b 5, lb 7, nb 11)		23
Total	(100.1 overs)	447	(for 4 dec, 39.3 overs)		176

Fall of wickets 39, 42, 263, 288, 355, 396, 412, 422, 438

25, 129, 141, 171

Bowling

Gough 25.1–4–103–5
Caddick 29–4–143–3
Mullally 23–8–65–1
Tudor 18–1–97–1
Butcher 1–0–7–0
Ramprakash 4–0–12–0

Gough 17–3–68–2
Caddick 11–2–45–1
Tudor 4–1–17–0
Mullally 7.3–2–34–1

ENGLAND

M A Atherton	c Gilchrist b McGrath	22	c Gilchrist b McGrath		8
M E Trescothick	c Gilchrist b McGrath	37	c Hayden b Gillespie		10
M A Butcher	run out	47	not out		173
*N Hussain	lbw b McGrath	46	c Gilchrist b Gillespie		55
M R Ramprakash	c Gilchrist b Lee	40	c Waugh b Warne		32
U Afzaal	c Warne b McGrath	14	not out		4
†A J Stewart	not out	76			
A J Tudor	c Gilchrist b McGrath	2			
A R Caddick	c Gilchrist b Lee	5			
D Gough	c Slater b McGrath	8			
A D Mullally	c Katich b McGrath	0			
Extras	(b 2, lb 3, nb 7)	12	(b 14, lb 16, nb 3)		33
Total	(94.2 overs)	309	(for 4, 73.2 overs)		315

Fall of wickets 50, 67, 158, 158, 174, 252, 267, 289, 299

8, 33, 214, 289

Bowling

McGrath 30.2–9–76–7
Gillespie 26–6–76–0
Lee 22–3–103–2
Warne 16–2–49–0

McGrath 16–3–61–1
Gillespie 22–4–94–2
Warne 18.2–3–58–1
Lee 16–4–65–0
Waugh 1–0–7–0

England won by 6 wickets
Umpires: D R Shepherd and S Venkataraghavan
Toss: Australia

Progress of the match

		Lunch	*Tea*	*Close*
First day	Australia	—	86–2	288–4
Second day	Australia	408–6	447	
	England		50–0	155–2
Third day	England	232–5	300–9	309
	Australia			69–1
Fourth day	Australia	146–3	176–4 dec	
	England			4–0
Fifth day	England	118–2	222–3	315–4

First Day

Different things to play for now, different from before, different for the two sides. With the main contest settled, Australia will have their eye on turning this into an overwhelming series victory, at the limit a 5–0 whitewash. England will be playing for what is sometimes called pride but is actually more important than that. The prospects for, and future trajectory of, the national team can still profit from a better showing against Australia, whether only a hard-fought draw or a late, unanticipated victory. A dead series? Never. The objectives simply get redefined. Australia and their supporters will certainly value it if the team improve on 3–0. And should England put together a victory, you just watch the euphoria. The Ashes lost – that's too bad. But England have beaten Australia! A couple of people I know, neither of them close to cricket, said to me after the Trent Bridge Test: 'So they play the remaining games even though Australia have won the series?' You bet. And thank goodness. The interest remains intense. Speaking for myself, there's not only the fascination of how this particular chapter of the summer saga will play out, its particular twists and turns, incidents and talking points, heroes and unfortunates. If you're following the series at the scene of the action, as Piwi and I are, then it's also about coming back again to Headingley (and in due course the Oval), renewing an acquaintance earlier made. It's about getting the feel of the place once more as you arrive, specific in the way every major cricket ground is, with its own history and atmosphere, its own legends.

Ah, Headingley – the very name laden with memories, both personal and historic. Great deeds come rolling back. Steve Waugh's magnificent debut Test innings in this country, 177 not out. Followed by his 157 not out four years later and Allan Border's double century on the same occasion. Then Matthew Elliott's 199 and Ricky Ponting's 127, seen by Ian and me here in 1997, along with Jason Gillespie's 7 for 37 in England's first innings and Paul Reiffel's 5 for 49 in their second, culminating in an Australian victory by an innings and some. And then ... oh yes, further back, a memory of another stripe. On the Western Terrace, a drunken yob, noisy and disgusting throughout a long day; falling over at one point and grazing his knees, but insensate, undeterred from his raucous shouting, the blood running down his legs, abrasions untended. This was with Morris in 1988. Anything else?

Piwi drove up to Manchester on Wednesday evening, staying over at our place, and we made an early start the following morning. The weather forecasts over the previous days had been as variable as, well, the weather of an English summer; but driving over to Leeds on the M62 we could be in no doubt about what this Thursday morning had in store. The rain pelted down out of a black sky throughout the journey. Bouncing off the windscreen of the car, the wetness of the road churned up by the traffic close around us, it gave me the impression of being on deck in a storm at sea. Wouldn't you bloody know it? Can't we manage even one Test out of five with uninterrupted play? Thus it still was when we arrived at Headingley. We decided to go into the ground anyway and see how things looked before making further plans.

The weather at once improves. The rain stops, the sky clears. Our Headingley morning unfolds. Despite some silly bureaucracy at the gate which first sends us from one under-used entrance to another, then allows Piwi in there but not me, although we are in adjacent seats, we effect our combined entry through the power of persuasive reasoning and walk around the ground to see where we can get a newspaper. We go by the rugby league ground, spectators sheltering in the stand and cars parked out on the field in front of them. What used to be the Western Terrace has been torn down and rebuilt. It definitely looks better, but will its mores be affected? And the atmosphere of the place indeed comes back to me. It is of a ground somehow more self-centred and parochial than the other Test match venues of England.

We find our seats at the Kirkstall Lane end. They are positioned roughly as at Edgbaston, on the deep-fine-leg boundary but a shade finer than we were there. We watch the ground staff at work and read the papers. The pitch information seems as variable as the pre-match weather forecasts. I read both that this is a good batting wicket and that there is a suspicion it is very dry and may start to break up early, giving assistance to a certain leg-spinner. I see Thommo down in front saying hello to a friend and signing autographs. Play, we are informed, should begin not too long after the umpires inspect again at 1.35, weather permitting. It looks as if it will permit, though there is the occasional reversion to light drizzle.

The unthinkable happens, twice. His Great Cricketing Holiness himself, in full person and elevated laid-backness, passes us on his way out to the middle to participate in presenting Simon Katich with his Australian cap, and then passes us again on his way back. It is Richie Benaud. I mean Richie Benaud. And when I say he passes us, he walks down along the row in which Piwi and I are standing, and later back along it, and we make way for him both times with all due deference. 'How're you doing?' he asks, first time. 'I have to get to an interview,' he apologises on his return when I weakly attempt to get his autograph (Now that I think about it, I already have this from Bulawayo and the year 1957.) I feel as though we have come close to the magic centre of the universe, as with the many other devotees of this ancient ritual we stand and patiently wait at the place where the thing will happen.

The cricket began at 2.15 and the story of the day revolved around one innings and one partnership. The innings was Ricky Ponting's, a glorious 144, with an unusual prelude, which with a different outcome would have left his performance an unwritten blank. The partnership was between Ponting and Mark Waugh. It was not quite historic but nearly so. Australia won the toss and the stand-in captain, Adam Gilchrist, chose to bat. Katich was the only change to their side, coming in for Steve Waugh. Nasser Hussain was back captaining England, he and Usman Afzaal taking the places of the omitted Ward and White. Alan Mullally was preferred to Croft, leaving England with insufficient variety in their attack. The early play wasn't easy to read. Slater and Hayden began free-scoringly enough, giving a first impression that the wicket might not be all that bad, at least for starters. But things then toughened up, perhaps because the bowling improved. After several overs anyway, the Australian openers began to have more difficulty with shot selection, they edged and missed more and a breakthrough duly came. Slater was lbw to Caddick for 21 and three runs later so was Hayden for 15, in his case not only out but also down, as the ball struck him on the knee and he dropped from the pain of the impact. It was 42 for 2.

It might, however, have been worse. Between these two dismissals, Ricky Ponting edged a ball to Ramprakash at third slip who claimed the catch. The batsman hadn't yet scored. He stood his ground and Venkat, unsure whether the ball had carried, referred the decision to the third umpire. Everyone waited – and waited. The length of the wait pointed to the outcome; it had to be not out. What blossomed from so doubtful a beginning was an innings of

rapidly growing confidence and aggression. It was as if this
ground was Ponting's own, the memory of the hundred he
made here in 1997 helping to hoist him out of the mediocre
run of form he has had in the series up to now. He pulled
and he cut. Some of these shots were of a ferocity that
defied intervention. It was as good an innings as we had
seen this summer. Ponting came to his century with 11 fours
and three sixes. Shortly after reaching it he struck 12 off an
over from Andrew Caddick. Caddick was, for all that, the
best of the England bowlers in an attack that soon began to
look tired, discouraged and inadequate. While Ponting was
walking the walk, Mark Waugh settled in at the other end,
content to be in a supporting role today, though even in
that role Mark Waugh to the very fingertips. He reminded
us regularly of his incomparable grace of execution in send-
ing the ball to the ropes. At one point, indeed, I had a call
from Morris – who was watching on TV at home within a
couple of miles from the ground – just to enthuse over a
recent Mark Waugh boundary. It was a partnership out of
Test cricket's top drawer. The 100 between the two batsmen was reached with a Ponting six, Australia's 200 with
the 12 from that Caddick over. Soon afterwards I consulted
my *Ashes Handbook*, to find that Ponting and Waugh were
approaching the Australian third-wicket record for this
ground: 229 by Bradman and Kippax in 1930, when
Bradman made his 334. Alas, they were only eight runs short
of it when Ponting nicked a catch to Stewart off Tudor and
the show was over.

Martyn came in and he and Waugh now navigated steadily
towards close of play, but in the final over of the day Waugh
was undone for 72 by a rising delivery from Caddick, the
ball lobbing up to be caught by Ramprakash. It was a surprise in a way, because Waugh had earlier been severely tested
by sustained short-pitched bowling from both Caddick and

Gough, with close catchers in place on both sides of the
wicket. This certainly troubled him, and it produced the only
rough edge to speak of on an otherwise resplendent partnership. But he battled and survived it. Or he did then. The
ball which dismissed him was a late footnote to that spell. It
left Australia on 288 for 4.

We had been sitting, through the day, in the midst of a
group of avid Yorkshire supporters, people who knew a
thing or two about cricket. Attentive to the game, and ex-
changing pertinent observations about it, they were equally
attentive to what was going on in the match between
Yorkshire and Leicestershire at Grace Road. With Yorkshire
well-placed to win the County Championship for the first
time since 1968, a few of them decided, late on, to sacrifice
the Friday of the Test and go to the county game instead.

Second Day

Piwi and I set out from Bingley where we were staying at
Soph and Dan's and found our way to Headingley with time
to spare. On this occasion we entered the ground according
to the instructions on our tickets, which took us in at the
new Len Hutton Gate. Several former Yorkshire cricketers
have made themselves ridiculous, to say no more than that,
by objecting to the depiction on this gate of a contempo-
rary spectator group at Headingley; for it includes some
Asian women, and they, you see, have nothing to do with
Sir Leonard, even if they do have something to do with
modern Headingley and modern Britain.

The cricket today was not only less one-sided than it had
been on many of the other days of the series, it also had
more of the feel of a traditional Test match. The earlier
part of it was dominated by the game's second century, an
innings of poise and certainty by Damien Martyn. Though

this did not have the fierce power of Ponting's hundred the day before, its class was unmistakable. Martyn has a shot he plays through the off-side, which looks at first almost like a defensive push but has the force to carry to the boundary. We were treated to several. He played, too, a couple of straight drives just missing the wicket at the bowler's end that were an absolute pleasure. You could think of Mark Waugh or Greg Chappell for elegance and timing. These two shots belonged in that company. At the other end Martyn's team-mates each did what he could, none of them for very long. With the exception of Lee who fell to Mullally, they all lost their wickets to Gough. The best of these dismissals from a spectating point of view was Simon Katich's. He had played with some defensive care in his debut Test innings, quietly supporting Martyn's authoritative display. But eventually he misjudged the line of a ball and let it go by to clip the top of his off stump. Gilchrist also went before lunch, playing his usual expansive game and giving a difficult catch to Trescothick in the covers, who fell forward in taking it.

How Darren Gough is loved by the Headingley crowd. How they supported him today as he ran in to bowl to keep the Australian total, already large, at least within sight. They encouraged him, they cheered his run-up to the wicket, they celebrated his every success. The contrast with the England player who is still to establish his credentials and has not yet been accepted at Headingley could not be more stark. I recall some of what Derek Pringle had to endure here in 1988. On this occasion it was similar for Alan Mullally. He began the morning yesterday with a mis-field on the boundary, resulting in a four, and then dropped a chance off Michael Slater, although this did not prove costly. It set them off. Ironic applause has followed Mullally about whenever he fields a ball without mishap, and he is the butt of some rather ungenerous remarks. Today when he was struck for two consecutive fours by McGrath, he prompted the suggestion that England wanted to bring on someone who could bowl. Anyway Gough, the favoured son, was the success of the early part of the day for England and was saluted by his own; though, this being Yorkshire, Piwi and I heard one especially flinty character nearby insisting that Gough's five-fer was largely made up of tailenders. The record shows this to be not only not strictly true, but not even mostly true. Gough took the wickets of Katich, Gilchrist and – the last of the innings – Martyn. Martyn actually jumped down the pitch to him, serious aggression on his mind, giving a catch to Stewart via Atherton. Atherton could not hold the ball himself but took the force off it, knocking it up and across. Two numerical curiosities of the close of the Australian innings were that Martyn's dismissal left his Test batting average on precisely 50.00, a matter Piwi and I had been busy working out as things moved towards a conclusion; and that the Australian total of 447 was one I had seen Australia make before, at Old Trafford in 1989. Amazing or what?!

Early in the England innings there was a further oddity, in that we had an exact re-run of the catch-that-wasn't incident, this time affecting Trescothick. He edged a ball to Mark Waugh, in his usual position, and the Australians appealed for the catch. Referred by David Shepherd to the third umpire, the decision went against them, as had the Ponting decision gone against England yesterday. The England openers then stuck around to bring up 50 on the stroke of tea, but Atherton was out in the first over after the resumption, caught behind off McGrath, as was Trescothick very soon afterwards. With England 67 for 2, the question could not but occur, is this the great Going-Down-The-Drain Show once more? It wasn't. Butcher and

Hussain battled it out for an unbroken stand of 88, and while theirs wasn't any sort of batting display to relish, such as we had previously seen from Ponting, Martyn and Waugh, it was an England fight-back, as appropriate to the Test arena.

Incidental to the play we witnessed David Shepherd doing his superstitious skip-and-hop routine when England were on 111, the breakdown of the new electronic scoreboard at Headingley – which is an insult to human, never mind cricketing, intelligence – and the goings-on in the re-constructed West Stand. These looked and sounded much like what used to go on on the Western Terrace. Plus ça change. At the fall of the second English wicket, a prank-ster, one Karl Power, got through whatever there is of security at Headingley, to come out on to the ground dressed as an England batsman. He was too late, since Hussain was already at the wicket, so it was all rather pathetic.

Third Day

Our Headingley mornings have settled into a routine and we were again at our seats by 10.00. As Piwi went walkabout, I caught up with my writing of yesterday's events. Seeing David Gower stopped for his autograph as he passed by, I made my way over to put in a request on my own behalf, this time articulating the thought I had had when request-ing autographs from Merv Hughes and Paul Reiffel at Lord's and Trent Bridge. 'Sorry to disturb you in this way,' I said, 'not acting my age.' 'You don't want to do that,' Gower replied with a smile.

As is often the way at cricket, the dominant theme of the previous afternoon is found to have played itself out the fol-lowing morning. In this case England's stubborn resistance was at an end. Hussain was soon lbw to McGrath with only three more runs on the board, and without further addition

Butcher then ran himself out through an insane call. His straight-driven shot had had the pace taken off it by the bowler, Jason Gillespie, the ball travelling no more than a few yards beyond him. Diving to deliver it on target, Brett Lee assisted in the suicide. After a couple of attractive boundaries Afzaal then edged one outside off stump from McGrath to Warne at first slip, and it was 174 for 5. Unable to obtain tickets for this Test, some Australians have hired a contraption that enables them to perch on a small platform above the trees at the Kirkstall Lane end and watch the play from just outside the ground. They fly a banner with the legend 'Down Under On Top'. So the situation was once again.

The pleasures of a fine Test match morning ... One of them is reading the accounts of yesterday's play in several papers, comparing what others have made of it with what you thought you saw, their broad assessment and interpretation of detail with your own. Another, provided you are fortunately placed amongst spectators, is the sense of collective attention to something that intensely interests you all in common: the chance picking up and the sharing of observations, the information gleaned, memories confirmed, humorous asides. At Headingley we have been lucky in our closest companions. Today those of them who had gone off to Grace Road yesterday to watch Yorkshire playing Leicestershire were back. They cheered passionately when the announcement came over the PA system that Yorkshire had won. It was an unusual exuberance. They are low-key folk these, and pretty tough customers, dismissive of cricketing weakness, folly and lack of talent, quietly appreciative of quality, from whichever side it comes. There is also a young Australian in the vicinity and if there is a fact about Australian cricket that he doesn't know, it is as rare as the sight of no-nonsense Aussie cricketers showing sympathetic concern for an England batsman who is hurt.

Yet this is a sight we saw. Mark Ramprakash, who with Alec Stewart had taken England to 200, was struck on the wrist by a ball from Gillespie, causing a brief interruption while he was given aid and comfort. Lo and behold, some of the comfort was coming from his opponents. It warmed my heart, the broad humanity of it, reinforcing lifelong allegiances. How was it repaid? Ramprakash struck two uncompromising boundaries through the gully area to bring up the 50 partnership between himself and Stewart before lunch, and in the first over of the afternoon poor Brett Lee was mercilessly bludgeoned for 16 runs. That got England beyond the follow-on target. Lee's over was also Australia's 80th, permitting them to take the new ball. It was the first time in the series that an England innings had lasted long enough for this to happen. The new ball saw off Ramprakash himself for 40, giving a catch behind off Lee, his shot as unbalanced in the execution as the choice of it was unfortunate at this point in his innings. It also saw off Tudor, caught behind off McGrath. The latter had five wickets in an innings once again, and as he returned to his position in the field near the far corner of the new West Stand, he received the cheers of the Australian spectators there and the jeers of the rest, acknowledging both equally with a cavalier wave.

There was now an extraordinary passage of play, one minor drama following another in rapid sequence. It began with Caddick being hit on the left arm by a ball from Lee, and needing aid and comfort as Ramprakash before him, but not getting any from the Australians that I could see. He was bowled off his pads by the very next ball from Lee, to great Australian celebration – but it was a no-ball. Caddick was then again hit on the body and responded by smashing a four. At this point Alec Stewart decided to get in on things. A four off McGrath took him to his 50 and was the trigger

for some very adventurous hitting on his part. With only
the England tail left to support him, it seemed he had set
his sights on glory. He stepped back from his wicket – to
McGrath! – and cracked a ball over cover with such force
that it sailed into the West Stand for six. This shot was only
the most extraordinary of several Stewart improvised and it
was all stirring stuff, no doubt about it. However, the comparisons the following morning with Adam Gilchrist's batting
were off-beam. At this point in his innings Stewart was having what, as boys in Bulawayo, we used to call a wind (as in
'wind up', not 'Gone with the …'). Gilchrist, even at his
most forceful and enterprising, still observes the basic principles of sound batsmanship. The dismissals of Caddick
and Gough – Caddick wrongly given out caught behind off
Lee, Gough skying a catch to Slater off McGrath – and bad
light with rain coming in behind it put an end to the drama
and in effect closed the session. Tea was taken during a two-
hour rain break with England on 300 for 9. Their innings
was sewn up without too much ado when play resumed.
Mullally was caught at short leg by Katich off McGrath and
England were 309 all out, giving Australia a lead of 138.
McGrath had taken 7 for 76 and his 350th wicket in Tests.

Following an emergent pattern for this game, each innings
inherits an occurrence from the previous one. As Trescothick
was to Ponting with the catch that never was, so now, when
Australia began their second innings, Slater was to Caddick
with the dismissal that didn't count because coming from a
no-ball. Slater played a delivery – from Caddick as it happens
– on to his stumps and was spared, only to do the same to a
ball from Gough a little later and be on his way. Batting
seemed to be a chancy business out there, with the bat either
not finding or not middling the ball. Ponting was dropped
by Atherton off Gough, a high, hard catch had it been taken,
but nevertheless he managed a way through the difficulty to

recapture some of the stroke-play of his marvellous first innings. A pull to the on-side boundary brought up 50 for Australia. A luminous off-drive for another four won the admiration even of the tough Yorkshire contingent nearby. Then the light closed us down.

The game promises to go into the fifth day for the first time this series. Unfortunately the weather looks likely to assist in that.

Fourth Day

So, at three o'clock on Sunday afternoon, Piwi and I are sitting in the back of the Rugby Stand, facing the cars parked out on the field and looking at a downpour. Shades of 1997, Ian and me. At this point we've had only 22 overs of play and in a way I guess we should consider ourselves lucky, because when I woke early this morning the sound outside the window for a good hour at least was of no play, no way, not at all. By the time we left Bingley, however, it was looking better and play in fact began on time and in sunshine.

It began at breakneck speed as well, with 11 runs coming off Mullally's first over, then 10 off Gough's. Ponting was to his 50 in 52 balls and he pulled a huge six off Caddick soon afterwards. Despite signs of there being some difficulty in facing Gough from the Rugby Stand end, Australia had taken 55 off nine overs within 40 minutes when the first rain of the day intervened. The players were back on the field at 12.30 and the next half hour was better for England, yielding only 22 runs, this time for two wickets. The 100 partnership between Hayden and Ponting came up immediately after the weather break, following which Gough trapped Ponting lbw for 72 and Hayden was caught by Stewart off Mullally, the latter bowling a good spell after that costly first over of the morning. It even seemed to earn him some provisional acceptance from the Headingley crowd. After lunch, Mark Waugh opened up a bit, stepping down the wicket to hit Mullally to the long-off boundary, and Martyn fell lbw to Caddick. Then the rain returned not long after 2.00 and Piwi and I took up residence in the back of the Rugby Stand.

Time on our hands. Having read all I want to of the day's papers and grabbed a ten-minute snooze, I take a walk. I go up into the West Stand at a couple of different entrances, to sample the view and test the atmosphere. No thanks; been there, done that – a couple of times before. Even now, with less than half of its usual population, it is a place of drunks and exhibitionists. In due course the weather relents for a scheduled restart at 5.50, with 20 overs to be bowled. And shock, horror … Australia declare their innings closed. The shock, or at least surprise, is more or less general. The horror, so far as I can ascertain by talking to others around us, is only mine. I am not enamoured of this declaration. Notwithstanding the cricket history which indicates that it sets a testing target, and notwithstanding all that has become so clear during this series about the disparate strengths of the two teams, it is too generous. At 315 from 110 overs, it requires less than three runs per over. In the event, in the third of the 20 overs to be bowled before the close today, the gloom descends once more, later followed by more rain. The rate therefore moves up, towards 3.5 per over. It still bothers me. Have Australia gifted England the opportunity of a win?

Fifth Day

Back at Soph and Dan's last night I stayed up till two with them to watch Robert Rossen's *The Hustler*. It is as good a movie on about my tenth viewing as it was on the first.

There is a moment in his final encounter with Minnesota Fats when Paul Newman's Fast Eddie pauses to ask rhetorically, 'How can I lose?!' And of course he doesn't – not this time, hardened by experience. I picture the Australians, in their decision of the previous afternoon, voicing the same sentiment: 'How can we lose?!' Two ways of answering the question occur to me. You can get a bit too bloody big for your boots. And you can offer your opponents, all neatly wrapped and tied with ribbons, a target rate in terms of runs per over that would have tickled my grandmother had she but known or cared anything about cricket.

Here follows the tale of English triumph, by now desperately wanted against this, their best-loved but most resented foe, so longingly yearned for against the team they most need to beat, longingly with all the length of a decade and more under the cosh. Though Atherton at once announced the intention that should have been obvious even to Australia's fresh-faced stand-in captain by lofting the first ball of the morning to the mid-wicket boundary, he was out two balls later, caught behind off McGrath, the delivery a snorter and virtually unplayable. Too soon afterwards in cricketing time Trescothick was caught in the gully by Hayden off Gillespie. So England 33 for 2, and it was all just obvious, wasn't it? Obvious to the naive who live in the sunlit uplands, surrounded by benign and friendly facts and with no extended personal knowledge of the dark.

Yet it takes only a little imagination. Butcher and Hussain managed to steady things, then began to go for their shots, up to and beyond the 50 mark. One of these shots was a six by the England captain which led to a long, vain search for the ball. It had to be replaced. From very early on England were always ahead of the asking rate, soon comfortably ahead of it, the mileposts of their innings beginning to rattle by: the 50 partnership between Butcher and Hussain, the

100 mark, Butcher's half-century and – after the lunch break – the 100 partnership. The posting of this was followed by Butcher's taking two consecutive fours off McGrath to the deep-point boundary, and another pair of fours off Lee. He was batting superbly, in total command, and the game was starting to run away from Australia. The Headingley crowd, a fish of a different feather today, attentive, seized by a fervent hope, relished every movement towards the goal, willed the next step and the next, expressed its anticipation of the longed-for moment in unwavering concentration and support. The many Australians who have been on the Test grounds this summer were also here, and they urged on their team as energetically, urged them to find a way through, to stop the forward charge – as, surely, they soon must.

There was one stutter but only one. On 97 Butcher, who had ended his first innings with that humdinger of a run call, nearly self-destructed again. He was sent back by Hussain and survived the fumbled run-out attempt. More mileposts rattled by. Butcher's century, his third in Tests; the 150 partnership between him and Hussain; then something so far unremarked upon as far as I'm aware, that once their partnership exceeded 155, Butcher and Hussain had displaced the record England third-wicket partnership against Australia on this ground, set by Bill Edrich and Alec Bedser in 1948. Hussain brought up his 50, survived a confident lbw shout soon afterwards and was then out next ball, caught behind off Gillespie. This was out in the modern way, with everyone at once knowing for a virtual certainty that the decision was wrong. The partnership had been worth 181. With England still 101 shy of their target, a glimmer of light, perhaps, for the boys of the sunlit uplands.

Not this time, sport. Butcher continued on his way, and wasn't it just his day. Pragmatic, hard-working, confident;

mixing glorious strokes of more or less orthodox character
with some low-risk aggression over the heads of the slip
cordon – for, as always, when it goes your way, it goes all
the way, the flashes out of reach, through the gaps, not to
hand. Ramprakash slotted into his secondary role with a
fittingly pugnacious and scurrying 32, before being caught
by Waugh off Warne when the dismissal no longer mattered.
He and Butcher had added another 75 and the finish was in
sight. Just after bringing up the 300 Butcher cut a ball from
Gillespie with such power that it carried across the boundary rope for six. The winning hit – and this, too, had to be
Butcher's – was a three to just short of the deep-point
boundary. The crowd at Headingley, today a credit to itself
and the game it follows, too conscious of what was at stake
to indulge in the usual idiocies, burst with joy. It had come
about: Australia humbled at last. And by what a display, and
what an individual innings. We were to learn that Butcher's
173 not out exactly matched Bradman's score here in 1948
in at least somewhat similar circumstances, Australia chasing a very large target after a third innings declaration.

Piwi left immediately play ended to begin his journey back
to Hitchin, and I stayed for the honours and the chat. Only
one candidate for Man of the Match, Mark Butcher, for
what the Australian captain referred to as the innings of his
life. And plaudits all round: to the Headingley groundsman
for preparing the best pitch of the series so far; to the returning and now victorious England captain, Nasser Hussain;
from him to the crowd at Headingley for their support; from
him again as well as others, and recognised in the applause
from everyone still gathered there, to Adam Gilchrist and
the Australians for the spirit in which they approached the
finale to this game by the manner of their declaration.

All credit is due to England for the positive approach
they adopted to the challenge laid down, and for sticking it

to their many critics on the matter of self-belief and other such stuff. They weathered everything the Australian bowlers pitched at them, and on my reading this was not sub-standard. Lee bowled with speed and conviction and Warne put in a decent spell. McGrath and Gillespie both took more punishment than they have lately been used to, and they came to look tireder than usual, but this is in the nature of what England were achieving, not the cause but the conse-quence of it. There were minor fielding lapses; there always are in these situations. The general standard was what you would expect from the present Australian side. When all is said and done, England did the business, mainly owing to a magnificent performance by Mark Butcher. In bringing it off, they provided all assembled, including those of us who would have preferred the other result, with a great day of cricket at the very highest level.

Discordant Reflection

The uplift about the conclusion to the Headingley Test has been, so far as I'm aware, altogether general. Why, a straw poll of former Australian captains found them behind Adam Gilchrist's declaration 'to a man' (this according to a piece in the *Guardian* by Gideon Haigh). I am brazen enough to offer here, on the basis of the more limited cricketing knowl-edge of a mere follower of the game, my discordant view. In doing so I take back nothing of what I have said about the credit due to England. They did what was demanded of them in the given context, and with some style. The issue is with Australia's declaration, the most essential fact in defin-ing that context. To me this was so sorry a misjudgement that I have been unable to think of a single persuasive rea-son for it, or to locate one in all the post-match hoohah. I take the liberty of saying on my own behalf that the central points to be put in what follows are none of them based on hindsight. They were formed at the time of the declaration itself, argued in conversation with others sitting nearby at Headingley, and mooted with Dan and Piwi overnight, when the England innings was but a couple of overs old.

The decision to declare so early made no logical sense. If it was born of a confidence that, on the evidence of this summer, England could simply be swept away, then somewhat less than a full day to do it in should have sufficed, allowing Australia, say, 20 more overs to change the arithmetic involved. To knock over a house of cards they could have afforded fewer overs and the 'luxury' of more runs. If, on the other hand, Australia feared that England might actually survive to secure a draw, so that more time was needed to prise them out, more than just short of a day, then the existing arithmetic was laughable. Surviving, England must win. With the high scoring rates there have been throughout this series and especially with Australia's attacking field placings, slightly less or, as it became, slightly more than three runs per over was too soft a target. The draw Australia feared they contrived to make equivalent to an England victory, their declaration amounting to this one, 'You need do no more than bat out the overs.'

Did a worry about the weather come into it, as Adam Gilchrist intimated when the game was over? In that case he and his advisers seem not to have been party to the meteorological information available to your average punter in the stands. We had known since Saturday night, and the Channel 4 commentary team were broadcasting on Sunday afternoon, that Monday was predicted to be fine. Why was the Australian dressing room not better informed? Did the captain worry he might lose some further overs when play resumed late on Sunday, as it turned out he did lose them and was sensible to expect given the weather that had gone before. In that case the overs lost to bad light (as opposed to those lost to the rain which followed it) were wasted. They could have been used by Australia to extend their lead by a bit of a thrash, refusing the umpires' offer of the light, as the England batsmen could not, in their position, safely do. Or did the Australians misread the amount of help they would get from the pitch? This is possible. I was assured by one of the Yorkshire supporters near us, and this in the most certain of tones, that he had watched cricket here all his life and it was just plain unthinkable that England should go for the runs on a fifth-day Headingley wicket. I for my part knew they would go for them, having watched England through the summer and noted their captain's approach to the game. I also considered what they had to lose, which wasn't much, and what they had to gain, which was plenty. And, though no expert in these matters, I had formed an impression from the boundary that, even giving help to the bowlers, this was the best batting wicket we had seen during the series, an impression evidently shared by several journalists and TV commentators.

Against these considerations, the prevailing, indeed all but universal, wisdom seems to be that Australia wanted to offer England a challenge, difficult but not impossible to bring off, thus tempting them to have a go, and into taking chances that could help Australia towards a win. Now, such talk of offering a challenge is either a tactical concept or else it is sentimental claptrap. As the former, it was misapplied. The idea, as suggested by the phrase 'giving them a whiff of victory', is to set a target that requires significant risk-taking from the opposition, the risk, one hopes, becoming progenitor to mishap and error, and thereby finally to failure overall. But a whiff is what it is supposed to be, not a rich, warm, all-enveloping aroma. In truth, England had to take no risks. They simply had to last. Doing this with

Australia on the all-out attack would certainly bring three
runs an over for most of the innings, give or take some. As
it happens, England played more forthrightly than they
needed to, finishing with 19 overs to spare. That they did so
gives a clue to another element in the situation. They felt
they could succeed and played accordingly, with spirit and
confidence, Australia having given them a leg-up in this
direction by the softness of the declaration. The thinking,
'If they play positively, it gives us more of a chance', was
flawed from the start. It only works with a target that is
genuinely demanding, where caution has to be thrown to
the winds. I will take a lot of persuading that, with the run
rate as actually set, and the opportunity it held out of a
proud England success, Australia gave themselves a better
chance than they would have with England facing the following choice structure: *either* you plummet into a deep dark
hole; *or* you piddle around for near enough a day to obtain
the worse end of a draw. Teams regularly fold when faced
with this kind of choice and this kind of pressure. If the
Australian side avails itself of psychological expertise, as
something I have read leads me to believe they do, then the
purveyors of it ought to give some attention to the mental
and emotional dynamics involved.

Perhaps, however, the challenge theme is meant not in
the strictly tactical sense, but in a more open spirit, the spirit
of 'making a game of it'. Understandable – even gracious –
as this sentiment may be in the mouths, or the applause, of
those of the opposing camp, I have to say that to me it is
well-meaning claptrap. This is Test cricket, and it is Ashes
cricket – than which there is nothing more serious in sport.
It is not some festival where, you know, we'll all have jolly
good fun and the winning isn't everything. The winning *isn't*
everything. However, one of the other things, and part of
what makes Test cricket the wonderful game it is, is that you

don't give anything lightly. Victory only comes properly earned. To give the opposition 'a sporting chance' in any meaning other than offering them a very high-risk gamble, to give it in the meaning of really inviting either of two winning outcomes, this is cant or worse; it is the degradation of Test cricket to the level of the one-day game. It is too much Hansie Cronje – with no implication here, let it be clearly stated, of any bribe-taking component – and not enough Allan Border. As if the game and its supporters cannot cope with the draw as a meaningful result. As if fighting *for* a draw hasn't adorned the whole tradition. Woe to it, this tradition, if things are now to go the way of a 'proper', that is, a contrived finish. Gracious therefore – to repeat this point – as Nasser Hussain's remarks were at the post-match presentations, gracious in victory to speak of Australia playing cricket in the right spirit, Gilchrist's declaration wasn't part of that spirit, it was a mistake.

One may feel more affection, naturally, for a generous loser than for someone with his foot on your throat. Allan Border was better liked by his opponents when he was smilingly accepting defeat at David Gower's hands in 1985 than he was as the give-nothing, grind-them-down captain who followed. But it was this later Allan Border who forged the pattern of repeated success for Australia that has yet to run its course. Even if Border is now among those former Australian captains endorsing the Headingley declaration, as seems likely given where he is currently placed, I am certain, though I obviously cannot prove it, that he would not himself have made a declaration like this in the same circumstances. As player and captain, Border had known too much cricketing darkness before he succeeded in leading his team out into the light.

Questioned as to how he felt, for his part, having lost the game at Headingley, Adam Gilchrist said the result was disappointing, not the end of the world. This is true. It wasn't even the middle of the world, as my daughter Sophie once said in a different connection. It was a game of cricket, no more, not worth anyone's happiness or freedom, not worth a single injustice. To each matter, however, its own context. The context of this one is not the duration of the planet or the fundamental well-being of its inhabitants. Still, it might be said, even in the appropriate context, so what? The series was already settled; the Ashes had been retained. That is one way of looking at it. Here is another.

It concerns the place of current events within the afore-mentioned tradition, within the history of Test cricket. If you know anything about this Australian side, then you know about the sense of history Steve Waugh has sought to instil in it. There is their visit to Gallipoli at the beginning of the present tour. There is the campaign to be allowed to take the Ashes urn back to Australia as a tangible symbol of the country's now long possession of the honour for which Australia and England regularly compete. And there is, above all, the aspiration to achieve not merely victory, but a historic Ashes victory, emulating the 5–0 clean sweep of Warwick Armstrong's team in Australia in 1920–21. Or there was until now. For these Australians of 2001, what a waste! Not merely of the sublime batting at Headingley of Ricky Ponting and Damien Martyn and the unforgiving bowling, yet again, of Glenn McGrath. A position had been fashioned that was impregnable. Australia may not in the end have won the game, but they could not lose it. I mean how, Fast Eddie, could they lose? Other than as they did in fact lose, nemesis coming swiftly upon hubris, as it rightly should. But no, not merely Ponting, Martyn and McGrath's contributions in this Test, not to speak of the contribution of the rest of the team; but all the top-class efforts of a summer, all the outstanding cricket Australia has played. It is as if you had with the greatest of skill, energy and application, crafted something especially rare, especially fine, only to let it fall casually out of your back pocket. Australia had brought themselves to an excellent chance of a 5–0 result or, if not that, of at least returning home unbeaten in the Tests. This is now gone. If one discounts the chance of a second England victory, in the Oval Test, as improbable, they are looking at either 3–1 or 4–1. Not only, therefore, not Warwick Armstrong. Not Bradman's 1948 Australians either. And not Border's, on his second visit as captain in 1989.

The end of the world, when it comes, will happen and then, presumably, be over and done with. But history in the meanwhile lasts forever. At some things you only get one chance. Like a certain Greg of your country and your calling, you blew it, guys.

FIFTH TEST
The Oval
23–27 August

Scorecard

AUSTRALIA

M L Hayden	c Trescothick b Tufnell	68
J L Langer	retd hurt	102
R T Ponting	c Atherton b Ormond	62
M E Waugh	b Gough	120
*S R Waugh	not out	157
†A C Gilchrist	c Ramprakash b Afzaal	25
D R Martyn	not out	64
Extras	(b 10, lb 13, w 1, nb 19)	43
Total	(for 4 dec, 152 overs)	641

Fall of wickets 158, 292, 489, 534

Did not bat S K Warne, B Lee, J N Gillespie, G D McGrath

Bowling Gough 29–4–113–1; Caddick 36–9–146–0; Ormond 34–4–115–1; Tufnell 39–2–174–1; Butcher 1–0–2–0; Ramprakash 4–0–19–0; Afzaal 9–0–49–1

ENGLAND

M A Atherton	b Warne	13	c Warne b McGrath	9
M E Trescothick	b Warne	55	c & b McGrath	24
M A Butcher	c Langer b Warne	25	c S R Waugh b Warne	14
*N Hussain	b M E Waugh	52	lbw b Warne	2
M R Ramprakash	c Gilchrist b McGrath	133	c Hayden b Warne	19
U Afzaal	c Gillespie b McGrath	54	c Ponting b McGrath	5
†A J Stewart	c Gilchrist b Warne	29	b Warne	34
A R Caddick	lbw b Warne	0	b Lee	17
J Ormond	b Warne	18	c Gilchrist b McGrath	17
D Gough	st Gilchrist b Warne	24	not out	39
P R Tufnell	not out	7	c Warne b McGrath	0
Extras	(b 3, lb 13, w 1, nb 5)	22	(lb 2, nb 2)	4
Total	(118.2 overs)	432	(68.3 overs)	184

Fall of wickets 58, 85, 104, 166, 255, 313, 313, 350, 424

17, 46, 48, 50, 55, 95, 126, 126, 184

Bowling

McGrath 30–11–67–2
Gillespie 20–3–96–0
Warne 44.2–7–165–7
Lee 14–1–43–0
Ponting 2–0–5–0
M E Waugh 8–0–40–1

Lee 10–3–30–1
McGrath 15.3–6–43–5
Warne 28–8–64–4
Ponting 2–0–3–0
Gillespie 12–5–38–0
M E Waugh 1–0–4–0

Australia won by an innings and 25 runs
Umpires: R E Koertzen and P Willey
Toss: Australia

Progress of the match

		Lunch	*Tea*	*Close*
First day	Australia	66–0	203–1	324–2
Second day	Australia	440–2	580–4	641–4 dec
	England			80–1
Third day	England	158–3	259–5	409–8
Fourth day	England	432 & 40–1	—	—
Fifth day	England	118–6	184	

First Day

In the brief interlude before the fifth Test I decide to give up my cricketing superstitions for the time being. I shall abandon all those luck-inducing practices that have been in my armoury, silent mumblings amongst them. I pack different clothes from those I've been relying on throughout the series. I will no longer worry when an Australian batsman reaches 61 or 87. This has happened once before. In the aftermath of Headingley 1981, I decided that against exceptional human performance superstitions held no power, and forswore them. Little by little, however, they crept back and re-established themselves in my life. This time, after the defeat Australia set up for themselves on Monday, my decision to be done with all superstitious practices is differently motivated. If the people in support of whom you're making the effort can simply go and throw the thing away, why bother? I mean, what is then the point of it?

So it's straight down the Northern Line, 16 stops from East Finchley where I'm staying at my Dad's. The Oval, it again strikes me on my second visit, is quintessentially London. Not Lord's London, and not ladies and gentleman London; more your general populace and with a certain wide-boy lip. There is that sense, also, that the ground is somehow less divided than are others by the separate stands and enclosures. They're all there with their own particular names, to be sure, from Peter May through Fender and Gover to Surridge. But they seem to merge, as do their occupants for the day, making one common crowd all seated round the show. I am reminded, too, as soon as I take my seat, that behind third man in the Gover Stand there is no elevation vis-à-vis the pitch. Your eyes are about level with it.

Oh, these back-to-back Tests, traditional in Australia but a novelty in England. No more than two days in which to digest what happened in the fourth, before turning one's attention to the fifth. Shucks, I'll just have to force myself. Steve Waugh, who has battled his way back to some sort of fitness, wins the toss and says, 'We'll bat, thanks'. Michael Slater has been dropped in place of Justin Langer and England have brought in James Ormond and Phil Tufnell for Alan Mullally and Alex Tudor. We witness an old-fashioned Test match first morning. I'd nearly forgotten what one was like. The Australian openers play carefully, take time to settle in, establish themselves. On the hour of midday they have scored 40 from 13 overs. There is early move-ment of the ball for the England bowlers, and Hayden and Langer do well to negotiate it. A streaky shot by Hayden through the slips brings up the 50. At 12.30 there is a 15-minute break for light rain falling out of a humid August stew. Then Hayden and Langer proceed as cautiously as before to 66 by lunch.

Returning, they bring up the 100 in the 31st over. Phil Tufnell has come on to bowl and I'm glad to see him back. I don't mean from a partisan point of view. I like to watch him. He bowls with individuality and sparkle – whatever his figures today. Hayden and Langer both reach their 50s, the latter with a six over mid-wicket off Tufnell. The two of them are abreast momentarily, on 58 each, normal run-scoring service having been resumed since lunch. The Australian total is doubled well within the hour. There is then another rain break, this time of 20 minutes, following which Langer posts 150 for the opening partnership with a four through the covers. Hayden is caught at square leg by Trescothick off Tufnell and visibly annoyed with himself, for by now it is clear that there are runs in this wicket. It was a bad toss to lose. With spin at both ends for a short spell, Ormond bowling off-breaks, Langer plays without a hel-met. When Ormond reverts to fast-medium, Ricky Ponting pulls him twice through mid-wicket to the boundary. Whatever was Ponting's problem earlier in the series, he has plainly put it behind him. Australia go to tea having passed 200 for the loss of only one wicket.

During the interval I accost an obvious visitor from Down Under, introducing myself as a non-Australian Aussie supporter. I ask what he thought of the declaration at Headingley, and what other Australians he knows thought of it. He tells me he is one of a party of 40 and they were all fine with it. I sketch my arguments. Yeah, well, but he and the rest of the party all felt it was OK. Hmm, I must just have an eccentric view, I say, and thank him by way of concluding the conversation. He's too polite to concur. Ah, he's sure there must be as many who share my view.

After tea Justin Langer goes to his century in style. No nervous nineties for him. From 88, it's a four to bring up the 50 partnership with Ponting, and then two more square of the wicket, one on each side. He is overjoyed. We have seen some special hundreds from Australia this series. Though it has had its fine moments, this one isn't in their class: not of Mark Waugh's at Lord's, or of Ponting's and Martyn's at Headingley. But after the summer Langer has had sitting on the sidelines, it is a splendid way to return, meeting the needs of his team as Michael Slater kept failing to after Edgbaston. His achievement is immediately followed by misfortune, however. Failing to evade a sharply lifting ball from Caddick, Langer is hit on the helmet directly over his temple and drops like a stone. Evidently in trouble, he is helped from the field, retiring hurt. That brings the return of Mark Waugh, cool as ever. Waugh has enjoyed a very good series and I've relished it, I must say. There are few batsmen I'm more keen to watch, and he makes taking a catch at slip, whether straightforward or difficult, look like something advertisers should consider paying for, to give their product the stamp of true class. In 1997 I waited patiently but in vain for *the* Mark Waugh innings. This time he has delivered in spades. As it is almost certainly his last tour of England, he chose his series well. Marky Mark – not long ago, but now.

Ponting duly reaches his half-century. Some flag-waving Aussies not far from us have the stick from their flag confiscated by a steward and cannot wave it with quite the same flair as before. Like many others in the late afternoon crowd they are making one hell of a drunken racket. Ponting nicks a ball to Atherton, giving Ormond – obviously delighted – his first Test wicket. The little Tasmanian has made 62. In his three innings since Trent Bridge he has taken his batting average for the series from 12 to just over 42, about where it was when the series started. Steve Waugh comes to the wicket, to respectful applause. It is no more than that, respectful, but a welcome change nonetheless from what he got on his last departure, at Trent Bridge. The 300 is reached with a square-driven four by Mark Waugh, there is a minor scare for him when he narrowly escapes being run out in not quite an action replay of his dismissal at Lord's, and with eight overs left to bowl Australia are offered the light and take it. 324 for 2. Can't complain.

Second Day

Four years ago, for the last Ashes Test here, Ian and I came expecting a traditional Oval wicket, full of runs, and got something very different. By the end of the second day 23 wickets had fallen for an average of not quite 20 apiece and the game was over inside three days. (You can read about this in a terrific book about that series, *Ashes '97: Two Views from the Boundary*, by ... er ... Norman Geras and Ian Holliday.) This time the Oval has delivered on its debt to me and with plenty to spare. After two days Piwi and I have seen 721 runs scored for five men out. That is 144 per wicket so far.

The contours are of a runs mountain and so too are the details. However, like yesterday, today got off to a slow and cautious start by the standards of this series. Our view of it was from Surridge North, with somewhat more elevation than in the Gover Stand and at rather wider third man. Mark Waugh was dropped first thing off Caddick by Butcher at second slip – a regulation chance – and for some 10 overs the run rate was two an over. But after that it was back to business. Some highlights. Waugh hit Tufnell for a long straight six, the ball landing on the 'first floor' of the pavilion. A sweep for four by the other Waugh brought up the 100 partnership between the brothers. As this was their third century partnership of the summer, taking their tally from six at the beginning of the series to nine now, they are obviously speeding up with age. By lunch, however, Steve was visibly struggling whenever runs had actually to be run. Nearly everything that wasn't a boundary was limited to a single, with twos rare and threes out of the question. When 450 came up for Australia shortly after lunch, the partnership between the twins was level with Hayden and Langer's and about to become the biggest of the innings.

And then one of those sideshows that enliven the main story. The brothers are in tandem, with Steve behind Mark, the latter having started earlier and not carrying an injury. He began the day on 48, Steve on 12. But lately Steve has been gaining on him, more ready than before to lash out so as to avoid having to run for his runs. Two fearsomely struck shots, one square on the off-side, the other straight, bring him into the 90s, where Mark already is, poised on 98. Could Steve overtake Mark and get there first? Mark moves along to 99. Another boundary to Steve and he is on 96. Will they reach their hundreds in the same over, as would be entirely fitting for twins born a couple of minutes apart?

Mark Waugh in fact reached his hundred, his 20th in Tests, a good long time before Steve, who stalled on the threshold of his. Mark's second century of the series was not of the same class as the one at Lord's and it was achieved on a friendlier pitch. But it offered its considerable pleasures all the same. It ended in a blaze. Gough bowled him a slower ball which he smashed for six. The bowler then got a revenge of sorts from the first ball of his next over. It was a dismissal of an unexpected kind today, knocking out Waugh's middle stump; but he contributed to his own downfall by stepping away from the wicket to aim another mighty blow. He had made 120 and the partnership was worth 197. Meanwhile, his brother had been stuck on 98 for an age. He inched forward to 99, where he was in a position to bring up both his own hundred and the 500 for Australia with the same shot. He didn't, Adam Gilchrist attending to the other part. Finally, the Australian captain snatched a hurried single to reach his 27th Test hundred. Diving to make his ground, he took in the achievement for a moment flat on his face.

Gilchrist hit a six off Tufnell which was nonchalantly caught by a bloke in the crowd, and then Waugh followed up with two of those off-side boundaries of the not-a-man-move variety. He was batting like he meant it. I wondered whether, on top of your basic Steve Waugh, and on top of any pain he might be feeling, there wasn't in some of these shots also a touch of the Headingley result and the memory of his send-off at Trent Bridge. Who knows? He was anyway reminding everyone of who he is, of the depth of his determination. Gilchrist was the one Australian batsman to miss out on a substantial score. He hit a full toss from Afzaal to Ramprakash in the covers, to be out for 25. Damien

Martyn then fell in with the more general pattern, feasting on easy runs. He became the sixth man to pass 50, a cheeky reverse sweep for four included in amongst them. By this point in the innings, when a shot wasn't worth four or better the game was virtually tip-and-run. England had all but given up trying to take wickets. The fielders were spread far and wide, as many as six of them on the boundary; auxiliary bowlers were in operation. Waugh declared the innings closed on 641 for 4. He himself was 157 not out, exactly repeating his score of eight years ago at Headingley.

Oh me, oh my, another premature declaration. I would have liked Australia to bat into Saturday morning, as Border did at Lord's, and again at Leeds, in 1993. They could have made 750 easy and maybe more, surpassing Australia's record for this ground and their record in all Ashes cricket. England would have had to be in the field for more than two days. In any event, on the evidence of their start, England will not be cowed. They had 18 overs to deal with and set off at a lick. Trescothick took 12 off Gillespie's third over and nearly as many off his fourth, and the England 50 was hoisted in the 11th over of the innings. Would the story be continuing as hitherto? Warne bowled Atherton with a big leg-break, the possible sign of a change of direction. Unimpressed, Trescothick went to his half-century. Ricky Ponting was given the final over of the day.

Third Day

The Oval Test often takes in my birthday, but on my one previous visit the game was over too quickly for the scheduled conjunction to be achieved. Today it is. Of course, I have renounced all superstitions, so I can't expect this to be of any positive significance. But I can still hope for good things to come about in the way they sometimes just do.

Like the first two days, the third continued sweltering, though there was a brief, cooling shower as I arrived at the ground. Proceedings began reasonably well. Trescothick was bowled leg stump by Warne without adding to his overnight score. The dismissal ushered in another morning of old-fashioned, battling Test cricket, as reflected in the scoring rate. From 29 overs England took 78 runs, a shade above 2.5 per over. Mark Waugh dropped Hussain, then on 9, off McGrath, who bowled a tight, economical spell into the second hour. Butcher was caught bat-pad by Langer off Warne, and in general the Australians were sharp as nails in the field. Hussain and Ramprakash put together a 50 partnership, brought up shortly before lunch.

Sunblock, sticky heat, shirt damp against your body. Birthday or no, today we are sitting in the worst company since the Saturday at Edgbaston. In some ways I find it even more repellent. The 'sociology' of it is interesting, however. This is a group of young men, in their mid- to late twenties, maybe nine or ten of them in all. Educated and articulate, they were at university together, and I reckon I might find their company as individuals at least neutral if not congenial. They are probably nice to their mothers. But as a collectivity and at cricket ... to borrow one of Jack Nicholson's memorable lines, I'd rather stick needles in my eyes. Conscious of their number and the relative weight it gives them vis-à-vis everyone else around, these guys don't give a shit. They can be as unpleasant as they want in their enjoyment and feel invulnerable. So it's (all day) haw, haw, haw, in that loud, in-group way; it's homophobia and general sexism but, you know, self-consciously ironic – 'You can't be too PC at the cricket'; it's how much Dave and his new wife are doing it, and Rachel legs akimbo, and the particularities of someone they know going down on his fat girlfriend, and McGrath taking it up the arse, and on and on. In addition, cricket sensibilities here are of the pond-life variety. If an England batsman plays a marvellous shot or snicks a lucky single or is reprieved from a confident lbw shout, or if an Australian mis-fields or stumbles, it's all one: cheer, jeer, sneer. They hate everything Australian with a loathing that beggars belief, or maybe they just affect to, mocking not only Australia's cricketers but also its accents, its locutions, the lot. The great Australian players in front of them? Forget it – the enemy. And yet on some level they do know what's what. 'The atmosphere', one says, 'is not as good as it was here last year' – well, thank heaven at least for that – 'It was roaring'. 'That's because we're shit against these guys', his friend replies. Regret, but without any admiration or appreciation. The only let-up is when Premiership football begins mid-afternoon. Then they start to pay attention to the scores and to discuss them. You could imagine them – I mean the pond-life, not the scores – even human. I am a tolerant and understanding sort of a chap with a most forgiving nature, but as a very good friend of mine might say in such circumstances, did he not think it too mild, if these guys were to be visited with the most painful dose of haemorrhoids, I wouldn't consider it adequate recompense for this blemish on my Saturday.

Blemish is what it is, for the cricket continues as a most compelling contest. This is a wicket on which every dismissal has to be worked for, each batsman to be chiselled out. Just when you start to think it ain't never gonna happen, something does. Thus, Steve Waugh brings his brother on to bowl, and Nasser Hussain, soon after reaching his half-century, plays a ball defensively and it spins back off his bat on to the stumps. Australian delight. Perhaps because he is so surprised to have fallen to Mark Waugh, the England captain takes some time to set off to the pavilion, although not in any doubt about having been bowled. I start, somewhere around now, to perform my own very visible celebration of each England wicket, in full triumphalist mode: out of my seat, clenched fist, yay-hay and all the rest of it, including a policy of robust eye contact with my revolting companions: 'Chew on that one, boychick!' Tsk, tsk, lowering oneself to their level. You got it.

England make progress. Both Ramprakash and Afzaal play watchfully and well to bring up 50 between them and Afzaal his own half-century, until just before tea he hooks a short-pitched delivery from McGrath, it soars towards Gillespie down in front of us – now long leg to the left-hander – and you can see from the fielder's initial reaction that the catch is on. Will he complete it? The ball takes its time (only seconds actually but the uncertainty seems to prolong things), and Gillespie makes the catch. Yeah, Aussie, go – and up yours, shitheads. After tea Ramprakash reaches his 50, and then the new ball is taken, producing consecutive fours from him and the 300 for England. Meanwhile, we wait and we wait, or at any rate I do – since the dismissal of Butcher before lunch, which was Warne's 399th Test wicket, for his 400th. He has bowled away, with only the odd short rest here and there, and he is soon brought back on again, the new ball notwithstanding. Will he get there today? Of course, he must. He does: Stewart caught Gillespie bowled Warne 29. One or two of the denizens of the pond are influenced by the normal generosity of the rest of the Oval crowd to applaud. 'What?! Why are we doing it?' 'It's a historic moment', volunteers a less degraded member of the group, possibly recalling some link he has on other days with a higher form of existence. 'But it's not *our* historic moment.' No, it isn't. That'll be the dose of piles when it comes, sunshine. Yes, I know, I've given up on superstitions. Still, I can dream, can't I?

Warne went on to trap Caddick lbw first ball and was not only on a hat trick for the second time in the series but also had five wickets in the innings. Ormond foiled the hat trick to stick around for a while and Australia's grip slackened. Four overthrows were conceded – to riotous celebration on my right – and Ramprakash hit successive fours off Warne. He was at last playing the innings he so badly needed: persevering, responsible, maintaining command; trying all he could for once to convert a useful 30 or 40 into something that would really register. Ormond was in due course bowled, becoming Warne's sixth victim. And, strange turn of events, I began to communicate with my unlovely neighbours. One was wondering if any team had ever had to follow on after making more than 400. I wasn't completely certain of the answer but I imagined so and volunteered this. Another wanted to know how many overs there were left to bowl today, so I shared with him the information available on the scoreboard. A Habermasian ethic of discursive inclusivity applies also to people like these, I suppose. 'You're cheering for Australia,' the how-many-overs guy half asked and half observed; 'Why?' 'Because I'm a colonial', I said, wanting to add, 'and because of people like you and your friends'. It wouldn't have been true or honest, though. I would support Australia even in face of a wholly angelic England crowd. It's bedrock. 'But you live here?' 'Yes.'

Anyway, there was now a point of unity between me and my co-discussants. We all wanted Ramprakash to get his hundred. In my case, this accorded with a convention Ian and I had adopted in 1997, by which an opposing batsman who passes 94 has earned that much support – to his hundred, no more. But I was keen for Ramprakash to do it quite apart from this. He deserved to. At length he got there, to general acclaim and much evident personal relief, and with Gough batting in sensible support, England reached 400 in the penultimate over of the day. The follow-on target was in sight – no longer wholly out of the question. As Piwi and I made our way back to Hitchin, I rang Adèle. Some of the pundits, she told me, were reckoning that Waugh might decide not to enforce it even if he got the choice.

Back at Piwi and Alison's, I opened my birthday present from them. It couldn't have been better: Shane Warne's new autobiography. The inscription from them recorded that Warne took his 400th Test wicket at the Oval on my birthday. Bowling, Warney!

Fourth Day

On the morning of the fourth day we were witness to one of cricket's recurring dramas: would the follow-on be saved? Piwi and I had been restored to a position of relative privilege in the Fender Stand, with a vantage point behind the slips once more. England's score crept along until Gough struck a four off McGrath and there were 21 runs to get. It was looking increasingly possible. But then the key wicket fell, that of Ramprakash, caught behind trying to get a ball from McGrath away. With Tufnell coming to the wicket, it must surely be all over. There was a huge cheer as he survived his first ball, and he even managed to pick up a few runs, four of them from a boundary off Warne. Only 11 to get now; they might still do it. Finally, however, they failed. Gough played a ball from Warne defensively and it rolled back under his bat to Gilchrist, who had the bails off in a flash before the batsman could recover his ground. Australia had a first innings lead of 209. Warne's tally for the innings was 7 for 165.

All the while Piwi and I had been speculating on Steve Waugh's decision. Would he enforce the follow-on? The cloud cover today, we thought, might make it more likely. In the event, there seemed not to be any announcement about this, or else, as is more probable, we missed it. England were being asked to follow on, so they did. Brett Lee had the first crack at them this time around. Off the last ball of his first over, with Atherton facing, was that a chance or not quite a chance? I wasn't sure, but it sent Mark Waugh off the field for attention to an injury to his right hand. Colin Miller walked round the boundary to bring something to Lee, and today he was sporting green hair. Whether Atherton had survived a chance or not, his downfall soon came in the customary way, dismissed by McGrath, on this occasion caught by Warne at first slip. He received a warm ovation leaving the field, as if it might have been his last Test innings, and he responded accordingly, with a final turn and wave of his bat before mounting the stairs to the dressing room. Trescothick and Butcher then took the score to 40 before bad light and rain brought a premature end to the morning.

Premature end to the morning would have been a fine thing if that had been all. The rain took up occupation and settled in. Play, it was clear, would not be resuming for a good while. Lucky to be under cover today, we did what you do: waited, chatted, read newspapers. From a review of Warne's auto-biography I got this: 'I can honestly say I have never read a complete book in my life'. Spin 'em out of town, Shane – as one of a group of young Australians behind us had earlier exhorted his illustrious compatriot. From the same group now came a lament about how the weather can sometimes 'bite you in the arse'. By what would have been tea it was clear we had been well and truly bitten there. Piwi and I began to dis-cuss our departure: 5.30 if it's still raining then; soon brought forward to 5.00, with significant areas of the ground now visibly water-logged. And at 5.00, as it happens, play was officially abandoned for the day. It was doubly unfortunate the way things had fallen out, since Piwi had decided this was to be his last day at the cricket. He needed to be at home tomorrow to ready himself for returning to work.

In the evening we celebrated his daughter Gillian's birthday. I also studied a street map of Bulawayo, from a book of sketches of the town which Alison had acquired on a recent trip to Zimbabwe. The map had an odd effect on me. Something to do with an acute, breath-catching familiarity, combined with being brought face to face with the gaps that have opened up in my memory. A simple sheet of paper with lines and names – a place at once so vivid and so distant. North End, where I grew up, how small it was! And here is the street I lived in when I made my first acquaintance with cricket. It was, on the other hand, from a point marked on this map that I once went fishing, and once is the number of times in my life I have done that. So enough misty-eyed digression.

Fifth Day

The final day dawns fine. Final day of the match. Final day of the series. I'm back in the Fender Stand. On my own, I strike up a low-frequency sort of companionship with the guy next to me. He watches my bag when I go for a walk, and I his similarly. An occasional query or remark relating to the play passes between us. The Oval is more sparsely populated at the start than on any of the previous mornings but for a fifth-day crowd this is not at all bad. And it knows the civilities. Steve Waugh and his team receive a long enthusiastic ovation, as proper to the occasion and the quality of cricket they have played these past two months. Butcher and Trescothick, following them out, are greeted even more warmly. I soak up every detail with the sunshine. One such detail is that Mark Waugh, who had to leave the field yesterday after sustaining the injury to his right hand, is back out there with the hand strapped up, though not placed in close-catching positions.

The character and tempo of the game are about to change. The main question, of course, is whether England will be able to see out the day for a draw. Put otherwise, it is which of two sequences is going to prevail: that in which, since the beginning of the Australian Supremacy in 1989, England haven't lost to Australia at the Oval; or this other one, that during the same period the fifth Test of every series has been won by Australia in a run of six straight victories. The answer comes quicker than anyone could have expected. Up to this point, 15 wickets have fallen in the match at an average of 74 runs each. Now England lose three wickets in five overs and five balls for only 10. Butcher is first to go, caught at short leg by Steve Waugh off Warne. Then Trescothick is dropped at slip by Ponting off McGrath but the miss is as costless as they come, for the very next ball McGrath gets one to snort, and maybe even bare its teeth, Trescothick knows squat about where it's going after fending it off with the top of his bat handle or glove, and the bowler completes the return catch in triumph and relief. Hussain is the day's third victim, lbw to Warne. Some brief resistance follows before Afzaal is taken brilliantly off McGrath by Ponting at second slip, falling in front of Warne at first. England are 15 for 4 on the morning so far and 55 for 5 all told. Their innings is in ruins.

Something of a stand, however, now develops between Stewart and Ramprakash. Entirely moderate in my impatience, I say to myself that if we can get rid of one of these two before lunch we'll *really* be on our way. Some Aussie supporters in the Peter May Enclosure are calling out to the Australian players in turn, 'McGrath give us a wave', 'Dizzy give us a wave' and so on, and generally getting a co-operative response. But having evidently met with a more stubborn one, they direct a modified call to Adam Gilchrist on the subject of his neighbour at first slip: 'Hey Gilly, make Warney wave'. The Australian wicket-keeper has a word, but it's no go from Warney. A big stage shrug by Gilchrist to the relevant quarter of the ground – 'What can I do? The great man has his reasons'. For this lack of responsiveness the great man in question is immediately rewarded with another wicket. It is that of Ramprakash, caught by Matthew Hayden at slip, from a ball firmly cut and seemingly past him when his hands close on it. This moves Warne above Curtly Ambrose into fifth spot among the all-time highest Test wicket-takers. Alec Stewart manages to get England past the 100 with a streaky near-chance through the slips, but when lunch arrives everyone knows it's now only a matter of time.

Even this began to look like an exaggeration with the master spinner operating at his best after the interval. He worried away at Stewart, England's one remaining batsman, putting him to the test to judge the line, the bounce, the variation of each delivery. You could see the effort of concentration that went into this. But it was to no avail. Off the final ball of an over, Stewart was duly defeated. He thrust his pad forward, allowing a sharply turning delivery to pass across it, and it hit the top of his off stump. Australia were now amongst the England tailenders, the first of whom, Caddick, was bowled the very next ball by a ninety-mile-an-hour yorker from Brett Lee. Thus concluded the duel between Lee and Caddick begun at Headingley. Although he has not had great success this series as a bowler, I have enjoyed watching Lee. The sheer speed and youthful energy, the visible delight with which he has reacted to each of the relatively few wickets he has taken, his just as evident pleasure in playing his part within the Australian side and the unfailing commitment in his fielding and throwing, have united to convey the image of a cricketer who really loves what he does. Whether he will develop into the top-flight bowler some have already hailed him as remains to be seen, but for now what he has displayed during this series suffices in its own way: a manifestation of the keen spirit in which Australia have played.

With nothing more to hope for in the matter of the match result, the Oval crowd had some extended diversionary fun with the Mexican wave. I guess we all have our forms of consolation for life's disappointments. Lee hit Gough painfully on the upper thigh, so that he had to call for the physio, dropping his trousers for some very public attention to the angry mark there. Whether induced by the crowd's frivolity or by the blow to his thigh and his dignity, he then decided he wouldn't bat like a tailender and just have a tonk; he would play as if to save the game. Ormond likewise. They defended – more effectively than those who had come before. It couldn't last, of course. But it did. And then some more. It came about indeed that Gough took two fours off McGrath to seal a partnership of 50 between Ormond and himself. Tea was approaching. Was this possible? Were Gough and Ormond going to extend their stay into the final session and begin to really worry … people? Don't be silly. McGrath finished it: Ormond caught by Gilchrist and Tufnell caught by Warne. At the death, victory for Australia by an innings and 25 runs.

McGrath and Warne, Warne and McGrath. Between them they had accounted for 18 of England's 20 wickets. McGrath took 5 for 43 in the second innings, overhauling Dennis Lillee's total of 355 Test wickets in the process and being chosen as Australia's Man of the Series. Warne was Man of the Match. How fitting that these two should be England's final destroyers here. It put the lid on their combined performance over the summer, with 32 wickets in all for McGrath and 31 for Warne. If you wanted a display of sheer professional skill, you could not find better than the dismantling of their opponents by this deadly duo on the final day. At the closing ceremony, in which Mark Butcher was nominated England's Man of the Series, England, through his words and those of their captain Nasser Hussain, were generous in defeat, Australia, through Steve Waugh, magnanimous in victory. The crowd, too, excelled itself in the generosity of its response. Australia did their final lap of honour, having earned every accolade. They are on their way home, and you just saw one of the greatest of teams, Frank Keating, playing cricket like you dream it, cricket to emblazon for the thing of wonder it can be.

As always, there are the end-of-summer thoughts: first amongst these the thought of those who won't be seen again on the Test grounds of England. For Australia, this is certainly true of Steve and Mark Waugh, and it may also be true of Warne and McGrath. Of them, given what I have written here already, suffice to say they have been giants, an unforgettable pleasure to have seen. But mention there should also be of Michael Atherton's departure from the Test arena and Alec Stewart's possible departure. Both of them are batsmen I have generally wanted to see the back of, but only in the walking-towards-the-pavilion sense. Admiration for them is compelled by their records, and arises also out of the manner in which they have played and the different characters their play has expressed. Atherton's sticking power became legendary, his sheer bloody-minded concentration and courage in the face of everything whatever. And whenever Stewart came in to bat, I always had the thought: is this one of the occasions when the bowlers will stop knowing where or how to bowl to him? An innings of 87 at Trent Bridge in 1997 typifies him for me. Though it neither won nor saved the game for England, it had all of Stewart's explosive power. With batting averages below 40, neither Atherton nor Stewart will go down in the proverbial annals as amongst the greatest batsman in international cricket. Anyone who witnessed what they for so long were, however, for themselves and for their country, will feel regret as – or, in Stewart's case, when – they go.

Back in Manchester, I took the trouble to look out an answer to that question from my pondly neighbour. Has any team ever had to follow on after making more than 400? I cannot be sure of the comprehensiveness of my researches on this point, but what I came up with were at least three previous occasions: Australia against England at Nottingham in 1938, after making 411 to England's 658 for 8 declared; India against the West Indies at Feroz Shah Kotla in 1948–49, after making 454 in reply to West Indies' 631 (a deficit which would not have allowed the follow-on under present rules); and New Zealand against Pakistan at Auckland in 1988–89, having scored 403 in their first innings to Pakistan's 616 for 5 declared. These games were all drawn. Consequently, if they are the only instances, then England at the Oval in 2001 were the first team to follow on after making more than 400, and then lose the game. This was, in any case, Australia's first victory at the Oval, not just during the Australian Supremacy, but since 1972. Less noticed was the sequence I have already alluded to: that is, of consecutive wins by Australia in the fifth Test of the series. This sequence now runs to eight, in fact. You have to go back to Edgbaston in 1985 to find an England win in that spot. OK, OK, I know. What person with a normally balanced set of preoccupations *would* notice a thing like this?

During the presentations at the Oval, Steve Waugh was asked by Dermot Reeve whether he felt the scoreline of 4–1 was a fair reflection of the gulf between the two teams. Waugh side-stepped the question, but here is my answer: no, it wasn't. Only a scoreline ending in zero, either 4- or 5–0, would have represented the disparity adequately. England would not have had a single victory against Australia without the 'assist' of Australia's declaration at Headingley. As Nasser Hussain realistically acknowledged in an unstinting remark during the same ceremony, England were playing against a team superior in every department of the game. One index of that superiority was that across the Tests of this summer Australia averaged, for every wicket lost, very nearly a half-century partnership: 49.1, to be precise. Which is to say that they were batting close to 500 an innings for an entire series. In none of the Tests did England manage to bowl them out twice. If it is true that one can sometimes be overawed by the immediacy of what is before you, so that things lying further back diminish by comparison, there is also in this particular domain – the love and the memory of sport – another, and I would say more prevalent, danger. It is the besetting temptation of nostalgia and age: that the figures of the present cannot possibly match the heroes of the past. This is a view constantly held and constantly falsified. Just as it would have prevented you from recognising the greatness of a Sobers, a Graeme Pollock, a Lillee, a Gavaskar or a Botham, so now it can be used to belittle the record or begrudge the stature of a remarkable team. Who cares whether or not this Australia were the greatest ever? They were great enough. As Christopher Martin-Jenkins wrote at the conclusion of this Oval Test, they were even stronger than the Australian sides which had won the previous six series against England – and that is saying something – their victory here 'silencing any lingering voices of doubt about their exalted place in history.'

Differently expressed: a funky bunch. This team, my team – by adoption, to be sure, but an adoption of very long standing now – won. It makes a difference, as the majority of those who follow sport well know. I would have enjoyed things less had Australia lost. Even so, this is only a part of the summer holiday now ended. The rest of the experience is something which endures across the specificities of time, success and failure. It is the sitting together again with others and at rest. It is the common dedication, despite opposed allegiances, to a common pursuit and the values it embodies. It is the admiration of talent, character under pressure, beauty in movement, structured creativity on display. To each, of course, their own preferred variant, but that is one corner of any utopia worth the name – the pond always excepted.

SERIES
AVERAGES

England batting and fielding

	M	*I*	*NO*	*Runs*	*HS*	*Ave*	*100*	*50*	*Ct/St*
M A Butcher	5	10	1	456	173*	50.66	1	1	4
M R Ramprakash	4	8	0	318	133	39.75	1	0	3
N Hussain	3	6	1	177	55	35.40	0	2	0
A J Stewart	5	9	1	283	76*	35.37	0	2	13
M E Trescothick	5	10	0	321	76	32.10	0	3	4
M A Atherton	5	10	0	221	57	22.10	0	2	7
J Ormond	1	2	0	35	18	17.50	0	0	0
U Afzaal	3	6	1	83	54	16.60	0	1	0
A R Caddick	5	9	2	101	49*	14.42	0	0	1
D Gough	5	9	3	82	39*	13.66	0	0	0
I J Ward	3	6	1	68	23*	13.60	0	0	0
D G Cork	1	2	0	26	24	13.00	0	0	0
G P Thorpe	1	2	0	22	20	11.00	0	0	1
C White	3	6	1	38	27*	7.60	0	0	1
P C R Tufnell	1	2	1	7	7*	7.00	0	0	0
A J Tudor	2	3	0	14	9	4.66	0	0	0
A F Giles	1	2	0	7	7	3.50	0	0	0
R D B Croft	1	2	0	3	3	1.50	0	0	0
A D Mullally	1	1	0	0	0	0.00	0	0	0

England bowling

	Overs	*M*	*Runs*	*W*	*Ave*	*5/10*	*Best*
R D B Croft	3	0	10	1	10.00	0/0	1–8
M A Butcher	14	4	63	4	15.75	0/0	4–42
A J Tudor	44.5	7	195	7	27.85	1/0	5–44
D Gough	155.1	24	657	17	38.64	1/0	5–103
U Afzaal	9	0	49	1	49.00	0/0	1–49
A D Mullally	30.3	10	99	2	49.50	0/0	1–34
A R Caddick	177.4	24	748	15	49.86	1/0	5–101
D G Cork	23	3	84	1	84.00	0/0	1–84
A F Giles	25	0	108	1	108.00	0/0	1–108
J Ormond	34	4	115	1	115.00	0/0	1–115
P C R Tuffnell	39	2	174	1	174.00	0/0	1–174
C White	46.4	7	189	1	189.00	0/0	1–101
M R Ramprakash	8	0	31	0	—	0/0	—

Australia batting and fielding

	M	I	NO	Runs	HS	Ave	100	50	Ct/St
S R Waugh	4	5	2	321	157*	107.00	2	0	2
M E Waugh	5	8	3	430	120	86.00	2	1	9
D R Martyn	5	7	2	382	118	76.40	2	2	0
A C Gilchrist	5	5	0	340	152	68.00	1	2	24/2
R T Ponting	5	8	0	338	144	42.25	1	2	7
M L Hayden	5	8	1	234	68	33.42	0	1	4
M J Slater	4	7	0	170	77	24.28	0	1	1
S M Katich	1	2	1	15	15	15.00	0	0	1
J N Gillespie	5	4	1	41	27*	13.66	0	0	2
G D McGrath	5	4	3	11	8*	11.00	0	0	1
B Lee	5	4	0	24	20	6.00	0	0	0
S K Warne	5	4	0	13	8	3.25	0	0	6
J L Langer	1	1	1	102	102*	—	1	0	1

Australia bowling

	Overs	M	Runs	W	Ave	5/10	Best
G D McGrath	194.2	56	542	32	16.93	4/0	7–76
S K Warne	195.2	41	580	31	18.70	3/1	7–165
J N Gillespie	174	42	652	19	34.31	1/0	5–53
B Lee	120.5	18	496	9	55.11	0/0	2–37
M E Waugh	13	1	69	1	69.00	0/0	1–40
R T Ponting	4	0	8	0	—	0/0	—

THE AUSTRALIAN
SUPREMACY

Australia's results against England 1989–2001

match no.	season and venue	scores	result
1	1989 Headingley	Australia 601–7 dec and 230–3 dec; England 430 and 191	Won by 210 runs
2	1989 Lord's	England 286 and 359; Australia 528 and 119–4	Won by 6 wickets
3	1989 Edgbaston	Australia 424 and 158–2; England 242	Drawn
4	1989 Old Trafford	England 260 and 264; Australia 447 and 81–1	Won by 9 wickets
5	1989 Trent Bridge	Australia 602–6 dec; England 255 and 167	Won by inns and 180 runs
6	1989 The Oval	Australia 468 and 219–4 dec; England 285 and 143–5	Drawn
7	1990–1 Brisbane	England 194 and 114; Australia 152 and 157–0	Won by 10 wickets
8	1990–1 Melbourne	England 352 and 150; Australia 306 and 197–2	Won by 8 wickets
9	1990–1 Sydney	Australia 518 and 205; England 469–8 dec and 113–4	Drawn
10	1990–1 Adelaide	Australia 386 and 314–6 dec; England 229 and 335–5	Drawn
11	1990–1 Perth	England 244 and 182; Australia 307 and 120–1	Won by 9 wickets
12	1993 Old Trafford	Australia 289 and 432–5 dec; England 210 and 332	Won by 179 runs
13	1993 Lord's	Australia 632–4 dec; England 205 and 365	Won by inns and 62 runs
14	1993 Trent Bridge	England 321 and 422–6 dec; Australia 373 and 202–6	Drawn
15	1993 Headingley	Australia 653–4 dec; England 200 and 305	Won by inns and 148 runs
16	1993 Edgbaston	England 276 and 251; Australia 408 and 120–2	Won by 8 wickets
17	1993 The Oval	England 380 and 313; Australia 303 and 229	Lost by 161 runs
18	1994–5 Brisbane	Australia 426 and 248–8 dec; England 167 and 323	Won by 184 runs
19	1994–5 Melbourne	Australia 279 and 320–7 dec; England 212 and 92	Won by 295 runs
20	1994–5 Sydney	England 309 and 255–2 dec; Australia 116 and 344–7	Drawn
21	1994–5 Adelaide	England 353 and 328; Australia 419 and 156	Lost by 106 runs
22	1994–5 Perth	Australia 402 and 345–8 dec; England 295 and 123	Won by 329 runs
23	1997 Edgbaston	Australia 118 and 477; England 478–9 dec and 119–1	Lost by 9 wickets
24	1997 Lord's	England 77 and 266–4 dec; Australia 213–7 dec	Drawn
25	1997 Old Trafford	Australia 235 and 395–8 dec; England 162 and 200	Won by 268 runs
26	1997 Headingley	England 172 and 268; Australia 501–9 dec	Won by inns and 61 runs
27	1997 Trent Bridge	Australia 427 and 336; England 313 and 186	Won by 264 runs
28	1997 The Oval	England 180 and 163; Australia 220 and 104	Lost by 19 runs
29	1998–9 Brisbane	Australia 485 and 237–3 dec; England 375 and 179–6	Drawn
30	1998–9 Perth	England 112 and 191; Australia 240 and 64–3	Won by 7 wickets
31	1998–9 Adelaide	Australia 391 and 278–5 dec; England 227 and 237	Won by 205 runs
32	1998–9 Melbourne	England 270 and 244; Australia 340 and 162	Lost by 12 runs
33	1998–9 Sydney	Australia 322 and 184; England 220 and 188	Won by 98 runs
34	2001 Edgbaston	England 294 and 164; Australia 576	Won by inns and 118 runs
35	2001 Lord's	England 187 and 227; Australia 401 and 14–2	Won by 8 wickets
36	2001 Trent Bridge	England 185 and 162; Australia 190 and 158–3	Won by 7 wickets
37	2001 Headingley	Australia 447 and 176–4 dec; England 309 and 315–4	Lost by 6 wickets
38	2001 The Oval	Australia 641–4 dec; England 432 and 184	Won by inns and 25 runs

Innings above 400

Australia (22)

match no.	score
15	653–4 dec
38	641–4 dec
13	632–4 dec
5	602–6 dec
1	601–7 dec
34	576
2	528
9	518
26	501–9 dec
29	485
23	477
6	468
4	447
37	447
12	432–5 dec
27	427
18	426
3	424
21	419
16	408
22	402
35	401

England (5)

match no.	score
23	478–9 dec
9	469–8 dec
38	432
1	430
14	422–6 dec

Australia's results by Test match

	First	*Second*	*Third*	*Fourth*	*Fifth*	*Sixth*
1989	won	won	drawn	won	won	drawn
1990–1	won	won	drawn	drawn	won	—
1993	won	won	drawn	won	won	lost
1994–5	won	won	drawn	lost	won	—
1997	lost	drawn	won	won	won	lost
1998–9	drawn	won	won	lost	won	—
2001	won	won	won	lost	won	—
totals	5–1–(1)	6–0–(1)	3–0–(4)	3–3–(1)	7–0–(0)	0–2–(1)

Australia's results by venue

	Edgbaston	*Headingley*	*Lord's*	*Old Trafford*	*The Oval*	*Trent Bridge*
1989	drawn	won	won	won	drawn	won
1993	won	won	won	won	lost	drawn
1997	lost	won	drawn	won	lost	won
2001	won	lost	won	—	won	won
totals	2–1–(1)	3–1–(0)	3–0–(1)	3–0–(0)	1–2–(1)	3–0–(1)

	Adelaide	*Brisbane*	*Melbourne*	*Perth*	*Sydney*
1990–1	drawn	won	won	won	drawn
1994–5	lost	won	won	won	drawn
1998–9	won	drawn	lost	won	won
totals	1–1–(1)	2–0–(1)	2–1–(0)	3–0–(0)	1–0–(2)